THE ORIGINS OF
MODERN CONSCIOUSNESS

THE ORIGINS OF MODERN CONSCIOUSNESS

Edited and with an Introduction by John Weiss
Wayne State University

Essays by

JOHN HIGHAM

ALBERT WILLIAM LEVI

EUGEN WEBER

ROGER SHATTUCK

BENJAMIN NELSON

GERHARD MASUR

GEORGE GAMOW

Wayne State University Press
Detroit, 1965

Copyright © 1965 by Wayne State University Press, Detroit, Mich. 48202
All rights reserved
Published simultaneously in Canada by Ambassador Books, Limited
Toronto, Ontario, Canada
Library of Congress Catalog Card Number 65-10145

This is Wayne Book number 18.

Grateful acknowledgment is made to the Wayne State University Alumni Fund for financial assistance in publishing this book.

Contents

Preface		7
Foreword by Randall M. Whaley		9
Introduction by John Weiss		11
I	*The Reorientation of American Culture in the 1890's* John Higham	25
II	*The Concept of Nature* Alfred William Levi	49
III	*The Secret World of Jean Barois: Notes on the Portrait of an Age* Eugen Weber	79
IV	*The Tortoise and the Hare: A Study of Valery, Freud, and Leonardo da Vinci* Roger Shattuck	111
V	*Friedrich Meinecke, Historian of a World in Crisis* Gerhard Masur	133
VI	*Dialogs Across the Centuries: Weber, Marx, Hegel, Luther* Benjamin Nelson	149
VII	*The Declassicalization of Physics* George Gamow	167

Preface

This book has been written and published with the generous support of the Wayne State University Alumni Fund. It is one of the results of a Wayne State University Alumni Fund Research Recognition Award which was given to me in the spring of 1962, in my capacity as an assistant professor in the University's department of history. As part of its terms, the award grants a large stipendium for the purpose of holding a symposium of nationally known scholars at Wayne State, to present papers in the area of research of the grantee. This collection of essays is one of the products of that symposium. I wish to thank not only the directors of the Alumni Fund, but Dr. Randall M. Whaley, vice president for Graduate Studies and Research at the University, who has given his personal support to this undertaking. I also wish to thank the Alumni Fund for enabling me to do research and writing toward an interpretive study of the themes raised by these essays. Above all, I want to thank the participants in the symposium.

J.W.

Foreword

It is refreshing to review in this collection of essays how man has responded in the past to impacts of science and technology. We who live in a continuum of technological revolutions can benefit from a study of the intellectual, cultural, and social transformations catalyzed in part by the emergence of new science and new technology around the turn of the century.

Professor Weiss has performed a valuable service in inviting specialists from different fields of scholarship to analyze together various aspects of these changes. More and more we realize that an understanding of the complex forces producing changes in society calls for interdisciplinary discussion. The reflective essays in this volume recount from different points of view the events of two or more decades of readjustment between man and the environment he was changing, readjustments in his thoughts about himself and his systems of values, readjustments of his views of the nature of the natural world. The process of adjustment is not orderly, and may even be traumatic as was occasioned by replacement of the security of absolutes by the uncertainty of probabilities and relativities.

The intellectual struggles and gropings for new meaning, for new strength through conflict of ideas, for a new fabric of thought combining both faith and reason that are reviewed in these essays should give us courage. While being deluged with new knowledge, the product of successful specialization in depth, we now seek understanding about how to use this abundant knowledge for the welfare of all men.

Facing this reality, we are pleased at Wayne State University to have taken pause for reflection, to have given thoughtful interpreters of the past an opportunity to meet and to record their thoughts in these essays. The alumni of the university, in supporting this venture symbolize a continuing concern for the power of the intellectual process and a faith in man to be able to shape for himself and his children a durable and livable world.

Randall M. Whaley

Introduction

by John Weiss

To what is the external world external?
OLD STUDENTS' CONUNDRUM.

The decades marking the end of the nineteenth century witnessed a fundamental and widespread transformation of the intellectual and cultural life of Western civilization. The inherited principles and ideologies of the eighteenth and nineteenth centuries were transformed by new and subtle notions about the relationship between ideas, ideologies, and reality, and about the use and meaning of theories and ideologies purporting to represent reality. No field, from history and sociology to philosophy and literature, remained unaffected by this change. If the modern temper can be said to have been born, it was out of those decades-long labors of the generation of intellectuals who brought about this reevaluation during the eighteen-nineties and after. This generation was the great seminal generation of our time. To gain assent, it is only necessary to name some of the men and movements concerned. This was the generation of Max Weber, George Bernard Shaw, William James, Friedrich Nietzsche, Benedetto Croce, Henri Bergson, Sigmund Freud, and Marcel Proust; this was the time of post-impressionism, the new physics, symbolism, revisionist socialism, neo-liberalism, and pragmatism.

There is more here, however, than everybody's approved list of important names and influential modern movements. There is more here than the beginnings of modernism in all its apparently distinct variety. We have, in fact, what one might fairly call the origins of modern consciousness. For this first and most influential generation of modern intellectuals shared a new and similar understanding of the meaning, purpose, and significance of the ideas, ideologies, and theories their different work gave life to. We are, in short, dealing with a truly revolutionary transformation. The essays presented here were solicited by the editor and are attempts to clarify and define different aspects of the intellectual and cultural transformation of the late nineteenth century.

George Gamow's essay recounts the crucial event of the "declassicalization" of physics at the turn of the century. As is well known, new discoveries in physics could not be fitted into the grand scheme of the laws of Newtonian classical mechanics. Gone was the hope that one simple and brief set of basic laws of matter and force were the ultimate basis of all physical phenomena and the final reality to which all could be reduced. Science had lost its metaphysics. Science ceased to be the progressive revelation of a few simple and external laws of matter in motion and became what it has remained to this day: a pragmatic, hypothetical analysis, revealing tentative, if highly probable, generalizations. As generalizations, the results of science were not only subject to change but, because of the nature of evidence and the process of abstraction, could no longer be expected to culminate in a finally true, self-consistent, rigidly deterministic system of absolute law.

As Einstein himself once observed:

> Science is not just a collection of laws, a catalog of unrelated facts. It is a creation of the human mind, with its freely invented ideas and concepts. Physical theories try to form a picture of reality and to establish its connection with the wide world of sense impressions. The only justification for our mental structures is whether and in what way our theories form such a link.[1]

Only those held in sway by the ancient and seductive delusion of absolute and final truth would find this to be a weakness in science or a cause for despair. Yet the significance of the change in physics at the turn of the century lay in its revolutionary impact, gradually felt, on men working in other areas of thought. The burden of scientism, so oppressive in Europe since the eighteen-fifties, was lifted. One need no longer take the old ideal of classical mechanics as model and guide for all intellectual endeavor. Correspondingly, the transient, symbolic, and tentative quality of thought in non-scientific fields could be seen not as a fatal flaw to be eradicated, but as a quality inherent in all thought. Indeed, one could now claim to be "doing science" as long as one, in whatever area, regarded one's hypotheses as pragmatic and heuristic, and one's generalizations as true only as pertaining to special cases and unique points-of-view.

Above all, the natural sciences ceased, with the new physics, to be the ally and main support of the materialistic metaphysics which had seemed unassailable since the eighteen-fifties. If matter in motion was not the ultimate reality but merely a useful hypothesis for explaining some natural phenomena, one could legitimately reestablish equality of status for man's values, ideals, and emotional responses to his environment. From Poincaré and Bergson through William James and Ernst Mach the sigh of relief seems nearly audible. Nietzsche, for one, found great joy in being free to doubt the reality of both God *and* the atom.

There is, of course, nothing surprising in the attempt of some to leap to the opposite extreme, and claim the new physics as a support for metaphysical idealism, as Jeans and Eddington were to do later. For those whose work has lasted until our day, however, the main direction of the new physics was rightly seen to be both anti-metaphysical and pragmatic. Absolutes of any kind were no longer expected and were not found to be necessary for useful comprehension, not only in physics, but in history, economic theory, social theory, and philosophy as well. Through the new physics, but not through it alone, the central modern perception of "the real" found general agreement. Gone was the Newtonian realm of vast shifting masses of matter in motion never directly known. It was replaced by the infinitely varied, uncertain, and limited—but intelligible and directly known—realm of human experience. True humanism was again appropriate.

The decline of classical mechanics, as related for us by Mr. Gamow, therefore, had a vast and general intellectual significance. The ideology of scientism, having ended with the nineteenth century (among the wise), relieved those attempting to understand other kinds of human experience from the necessity of copying the natural sciences in any literal way. That is why the humanist, to take up C. P. Snow's complaint, may not know the second law of thermodynamics: he doesn't need to. At the same time we are all scientists now, or should be. In every study, from ethics to sociology, all must work from knowledge through hypothesis, evidence, and culminating generalization. No results will be held final, no permanent systems constructed. This is true because no discipline can encompass more than a tiny fraction of experience, and because new experience presents unique vantage points for viewing the already known. Moreover, new experience can neither be denied nor anticipated. Notwithstanding the current cant of the two cultures, the work of the intellectuals of the turn of the century seems to show that though there may be many cultures, or perhaps simply one, there cannot possibly be just two.

Albert William Levi's contribution to the following essays deals in part with the errors in philosophy which result from our failure to grasp the meaning and significance of the new consciousness of the late nineteenth century. He reproaches those who, in spite of all we now know, perpetuate false dualisms by insisting upon the primary or even sole reality of either matter or spirit. It is true that few nowadays put the questions in such blatantly crude nineteenth-century terms, nevertheless Mr. Levi is quite correct to detect at least the remnants of such a useless bifurcation of experience: "Existentialism has neglected a philosophy of nature in concentrating on a philosophy of man. Positivism has rejected a philosophy of nature by producing a narrowly restricted philosophy of science." And neo-idealist philosophy at the turn of the century was, at its best, designed to put an end to such either/or reductionism. As an example, one might take F. H. Bradley's well-known statement from *Appearance and Reality*: "I am driven to the conclusion that for me experience is the same as reality."

Correspondingly, philosophers showed a new interest in early nineteenth-century continental idealism. It seemed a possible alternative to the various materialisms which had dominated since the eighteen-fifties. But neo-idealism, as it has been called, deserves the hesitant prefix. Hegel revived was corrected by Kant. Few, and those few forgotten, wanted to revive the naïve theological constructivism of the Absolute Spirit. Neo-Kantianism was more compelling because Kant emphasized in a thoroughly modern way the contribution of the perceiving intellect to its perceptions and knowledge. Kant's humanism and his philosophy of science spoke to the central concern of the time, which was: What is the role of intellect in organizing and comprehending the data of science, history, society, and the various derivitive ideologies? Philosophy at the turn of the century was increasingly called upon to aid men's understanding of what became obvious: knowledge was not only collected, but somehow created by the mind.

It is hardly surprising, then, to discover what one might call our contemporary obsession with creativity beginning as a genuine concern during the *fin de siècle*. Roger Shattuck has taken this, in fact, as the subject of his contribution to the following essays. He tells us of the intense interest in Leonardo da Vinci during those decades and suggests that Leonardo's standing as the prototype of the creative personality was responsible. Consequently, Mr. Shattuck uses the work of Freud and Valery on Leonardo as outstanding examples of the felt need to comprehend creative subjectivity. And this need, one might add, transcended any one area of thought. The historian, poet, scientist, sociologist, psychologist, and philosopher, as I have said, were united by their need to understand the contribution of the creative intellect to its data of perception and experience. Symbolists and expressionists created a cultural revolution out of their attempts to break down previously held distinctions between subjective experience and objective reality—and it is not too much to say that art has been working out the consequences of this ever since. Certainly, one need not go as far as Nerval's: "I believe that the human imagination has created nothing that is not true." And yet, in every discipline, the temptation was strong. Where *was* the resting place between arbitrary self-expression and the mindless objectivity of literal description? Such a question bothered Benedetto Croce as much as it did any symbolist. The force of new discoveries in every area led to the conclusion that creativity is the selection and organization of perceptions and experiences into a responsible thematic unity of felt validity in art, and demonstrable validity in science and social science.

Leonardo's unique attractive force, Roger Shattuck suggests, may very well have been due to his twin genius as both scientist and artist. Once perception itself was seen as not "pure" but as in part an interpretation, the vision of the artist and the hypothesis of the scientist could no longer be radically separated. One might even speak of the intuition of the physicist. It was William James in his *Psychology* who said that "Every perception is an acquired perception." Without pre-vision, he continued, there can be no true perception—we must have some idea of what we want to see before we can see it. Otherwise, our minds would simply reel from shock; and thought, let alone creation, would not be possible. Valery and Freud found comprehension and creativity to be a complex mixture of subject and object.

The mood was general. To quote Mr. Shattuck's brief description of modern Western intellectual history:

> Cartesian rationalism congealed into positivist theory with its idea of science and history as a growing collection of facts that would reveal their own significance in the shape of law and order. . . . Next to this idea of scientific fact, romanti-

cism spawned a tradition that declared the only true values are feelings—the passions and inner responses that tell us what and how and why we are.... The old conflict between faith and reason gives way to a new conflict about the very faculty with which we should encounter experience: reason or instinct, thought or feeling, intelligence or sensibility.

The search for the unity of opposites found expression in Valery's great interest in Poincaré's studies of the psychology of scientific creativity. Increasingly, Freud's investigations into the relationships between conscious and subconscious life denied any literal interpretation of the distinct, fixed, and mechanical images he himself had once propagated. The unity of reason and emotion was fairly shouted out by Bernard Shaw, and Bergson's *intuition* as well as Dilthey's *Einfühlung* made the point in the social sciences. Few of the intellectual leaders of the last generation of the nineteenth century were willing to perpetuate the commonly accepted dualities of the dying century, i.e., will and intellect, theory and fact, art and science, and—overarching the whole—idealism and realism.

Historical reality, to be communicated, must be organized to excess by hind-sighted pedantry. This our seminal generation knew well, hence their (and our) fascination with linquistic analysis and the metaphysics of grammar. I have tried to define the stark and abstract outline of the lasting intellectual achievements of the *fin-de-siècle*. For those, however, who experienced this change, it was a true experience, i.e., contradictory, confusing, and with no perceptible separation between the irrelevant and the relevant, the unimportant and the important. That is why we are fortunate to have Eugen Weber's excellent study of Roger Martin du Gard's novel, *Jean Barois*. As Mr. Weber informs us, "No work of fiction provides a more faithful, a more deliberately faithful, reflection of the period it describes than Roger Martin du Gard's life of Jean Barois."

That generation lived through what Nietzsche called the "death of God"—the apparent loss, that is to say, of all previously held objective standards of validity and value. A frightening and confusing loss for all, we see it falsely today, that is, through the eyes of those hardy few who found it inspiring as well. The journey beyond good and evil may have been launched with the heady exhaltation of new freedom, but the black despair of the *déraciné* was always a traveling companion. As Eugen Weber reminds us at one point, there was no need then to wait for existentialism to say that man must define himself, and that he can do so only through commitment and action.

Correspondingly, the younger intellectuals of the day were obsessively driven by the need to revalue all values. Hence the self-conscious dilettantism and *poseur* aspects of the generation of degeneration, Wildism, and the yellow books. Starting afresh in a void, they could not but appear to us as erratic, perverse, and capricious. As with Jean Barois, one sought experience and avoided conclusions. What we see to be scientific and cultural relativism, they confused with scientific and cultural nihilism. Too often, they could find no support but self-support. Thus Barrès, as quoted by Mr. Weber: "Pending the time when our masters have reconstructed some certainties for us, it would be proper to stick to the only reality, to the self." With the aid of Mr. Weber and Jean Barois we can understand how that generation could be enamored of those most vigorous expressions of the *culte de moi*: activism, heroic vitalism, spiritualism, and integral nationalism. We can understand why Huysmans and Dorian Gray could become, if only temporarily, true culture heroes.

The agony of choice is all the worse for those who can make none, and yet the punishing variety of possibilities open to that generation had welcome consequences for ours. As Eugen Weber puts it: "It is clear enough that doubt over the possibility of arriving at unique positive truths made for skepticism, eclecticism, subjectivism, and that—paradoxically—the multiple assertion of subjective truths would lead to the preemptory assertion of pragmatic truths." Pluralism, a refined awareness of the use and misuse of generalization, and a willingness to subordinate theory to the limits of observation have been some of the benefits of rejecting the absolute ideologies of the nineteenth century. If for us it has been pure gain, however, for those who lived through those decades, the culmination was a sense of failure, the result, perhaps, of their consciousness of opportunities lost and choices never made.

The new awareness of the complex and ambiguous relationship between mind and its objects was bound to have consequences upon that great nineteenth-century obsession, the study of history. Gerhard Masur's article on Friedrich Meinecke tells us something of this. Meinecke, his teacher Wilhelm Dilthey, and Benedetto Croce may fairly be said to have inaugurated the most influential rethinking of the intellectual bases of the study of the past in modern times. Above all, these three did not wish the complex and tangled trail of human events to be sacrificed to the stark metaphysical visions of nineteenth-century idealists and materialists. For them, historical knowledge is man's knowledge of his own creations, and it cannot be seen as the knowledge of the laws of the unfolding Absolute—whether that be called God's self-realization or the laws of economic development. Hence Croce, Meinecke, and Dilthey affirmed the power of ideas, yes, but not the power of the Idea; the force of class conditioning, yes, but not economic determinism. They affirmed neither system and in fact, no system, but a constant search for the mixture of ideal and material motives in all historical situations as in all men.

Continental historians may have pioneered in the "end of ideaology" simply because European historical experience compelled them to do so. Certainly the most influential ideology of the nineteenth century, classical economic liberalism, did not fit the economic history of either Germany or Italy. When the neo-liberals at the turn of the century sought to modify the rigidities of Manchester liberalism, German historical and pragmatic economic theories were ready to hand. Moreover, both Meinecke and Croce were intensely interested in liberal nationalism, the major revolutionary force of nineteenth-century Europe. They were well aware that there could be no monolithic explanation of the complex of material, ideal, and group interests which thrust into existence the powerful, unified, and semi-liberal nation-states of Europe.

For some, the disbelief in historical ideologies led to a safe, if drab and literal, factualism which still finds too much approval in the guild of historians. Croce, Dilthey, and Meinecke made the wiser choice, and launched their extensive and influential investigations into the relationship between theory, hypothesis, and historical reality. Once the ideological absolutism of the nineteenth century was discarded, they wanted to know the correct use of general ideas in the study of the past. "The philosophy of history is dead," Croce remarked. All the more reason to be aware of the implied philosophical assumptions which accompany all but the most literal statements about the past. As Croce made apparent, the study of history is as non-representational as modern science or modern art—which does not mean that any of them fail to represent reality, merely that they do not copy it. History is not a block universe which historians try to know, it is a vast reservoir of available past experience from which the historian selects some tiny fraction which seems relevant to the problems set by his own time and culture. That which the historian does not call to life because of his living, contemporary need for it remains "dead chronicle," to use Croce's term. Nor is some vast abstraction called "history" ever to be completely known. Each new experience, and hence each new generation, brings with it a fresh perspective on the same events and sees new relationships, discovers new consequences, and finds, when needed, new facts to complete its understanding of what is not really the past but its own experience. As Croce states in *History, Its Theory and Practice*:

> Enfranchising itself from servitude to extra-mundane caprice and to blind natural necessity, freeing itself from tran-

scending and from false immanence (which is in its turn transcendency), thought conceives history as the work of man, as the product of human will and intellect, and in this manner enters that form of history we call humanistic.

Benjamin Nelson's essay on Max Weber carries these themes into the work of their best exponent and most influential practitioner. Much of Weber's work, of course, was devoted to illuminating the relationship between theory and reality in the study of history and society. His famous theory of "ideal types" is, in fact, nothing less than his analysis of the signficance and proper use of theoretical models, laws, and generalizations in social studies. Weber's theory purports to explain as well what we really do when we theorize about data, a process he calls forming an ideal type. As Weber explains:

> One gains an ideal type by (first) a one-sided exaggeration of this or that point-of-view. Then one puts together a wealth of discrete and diffuse particular appearances which are more or less, and sometimes not at all, ready to hand. In turn, these serve to build a thought-picture out of these initial one-sided, abstracted, and exaggerated points-of-view. In its conceptual purity, this thought-picture will never be found in empirical reality. It is a Utopia and it presents to historical work the problem, in every single case, of determining how closely reality does or does not correspond to this ideal picture.[2]

The great ideologists of the nineteenth century, Weber continued, made the error of confusing their theoretical models with reality. He included classical economists, social Darwinists, Marxists, and Hegelians in the indictment. Our generalizations, models, or laws—in short, our various ideal types—should not be used to construct a fixed and final set of laws about such vast and unmanageable abstractions as history or society. As Dilthey once put it, to ask about the extent of economic conditioning in all history is to ask a meaningless question. Historians can only tell us of the extent of economic conditioning in a particular event.

The past can never be totally known nor does it conform to a single model; it is a vast deep from which we select only what we think we need to enable us to understand and control our own experience. New evidence and new experience must mean a re-evaluation, a new selection, a new interpretation, in short, a new ideal typology. Ideal types, generalizations, models, laws—they are relative, transient, and approximate. Nevertheless, as Weber insisted, the knowledge they yield can be disciplined, precise, and of a high order of probability. The mind, Weber continued, confronted with chaos, finds it helpful to construct suggested thought-pictures (his term); in turn, this image tells us where to look and which evidence is relevant. Ideal types are heuristic in value, they are not endings but beginnings—as those who have read Weber's *Protestant Ethic and the Spirit of Capitalism* should remember but rarely do. As Weber himself remarked, his theory about theory was partly the consequence of thinking through Kant's theme: "Concepts are intellectual means for spiritually mastering the empirically given."[3] Would it not be true to say that Weber's theory of ideal types may be taken as the keynote of these decades? For on all sides, as I have said, relative and pragmatic conceptions were transforming the inherited and rigid dogmas of nineteenth-century ideologies. As testimony, one need only recall the way in which classical Manchester liberalism was being replaced by historical and neo-liberal attitudes; or note the replacement of (vulgar) Marxism by the more subtle revisionist varieties; or, for that matter, observe the correction, in neo-idealism, of the theological rigidities of the original Hegelian vision.

We are indebted to Mr. Nelson for reminding us of Max Weber's crucial role as critic and perhaps even modernizer of the doctrines of Hegel and Marx. Weber rejected, to return to Croce's apt phrases, both the false transcendence of Hegel and the false immanence of Marx. Nevertheless, Weber remained committed to the theme of the grand ideologies of the nineteenth century: the progressive rationalization of Western civilization and its causes. How was it that the institutionalization of economic efficiency, the rule of abstract law, and the bureaucratization of social and political institutions proceeded so rapidly and so far in the West? Neither the self-development of the Rational Absolute, nor the inevitable development of the laws of capitalism, appeared to Weber as anything less than begging the question by reverting to a presumed metaphysical structure not to be found in history. Weber's theory of ideal types was meant to replace such absolutisms, and to make the study of society mundane, empirical, and above all pragmatic. Social historians must study specific social groups with their unique interests and values, as modified and directed by their tasks and environments. Weber himself made a lifelong study of the way such social groups increased or held back the process of Western rationalization. This over-riding interest of Weber's has been obscured, peculiarly enough, by the fame of his studies of the social-psychology of protestantism as a contributing factor (among many) to the rationalizing spirit of capitalism. Nevertheless, Weber's lasting achievement has been to bring the pragmatic spirit of the turn of the century to inform and activate the study of society.

In intellectual history—at least as far as the modern period is concerned—only academic specialization is served by rigidly separating America from the remainder of Western civilization. For this reason, and because of its inherent excellence, I have been gratified to be able to include among the following essays John Higham's paper on American thought and culture in the eighteen-nineties. Those who doubt the inherent and unavoidable interrelatedness of American and European thought, can only be persuaded, perhaps, by a direct confrontation with, say, an Italian pragmatist, one of the St. Louis Hegelians, a British follower of Henry George, or perhaps an American Marxist. In any event, Mr. Higham was assigned the formidable task of sketching the intellectual and cultural transformation of the *fin de siècle* as it occurred in the United States. As is to be expected from an historian of his caliber, he has avoided another acrimonious and fruitless debate, that of assigning national priorities or first claims. Instead he has discerned mutual influence and national variations within what one might call a common style.

For details, let the reader turn to John Higham's fine discussion. Let it be merely noted here that he will find many examples of American thinkers who joined with European intellectuals in the attack on the closed systems, formalistic abstractions, and ideological absolutisms of the nineteenth century. He will find the essential modern and pragmatic attitude much in evidence—the attempt, using Mr. Higham's words, to "create meanings out of the flux of experience." The reader will also find neo-liberalism in its American form, the "decadent" movement in literature, the doctrines of heroic vitalism and the will-to-power, and above all, America's most impressive contribution to the education of Europe, the great William James. As we read the words Mr. Higham uses to tell us of his three principles, William James, Frederick Jackson Turner, and Frank Lloyd Wright, we will have no difficulty, I think, in grasping their international application to the entire generation that gave life to the origins of modern consciousness:

> James, Wright and Turner were in their own ways hardy, fighting men, full of the zest for new experience, in love with novelty and experiment, eager to adapt philosophy, architecture, and history to the ever-changing needs of the present hour. James himself struck the distinctive note of the 1890's by interpreting all ideas as plans for action and exalting the will. . . . Intellectually, their deepest affinity arose from a common opposition to all closed and static patterns of order. James's repugnance for a "block universe" is well known. "All 'classic,' clean, cut and dried, 'noble,' 'fixed,' 'eternal' *Weltanschauungen* seem to me to violate the character with which life concretely comes and the expression which it bears of being, or at least involving, a muddle and a struggle."

The Reorientation of American Culture in the 1890's

by John Higham

In 1894 a group of Dartmouth alumni asked Richard Hovey, a young and dedicated poet, to write a new college song for his alma mater. Dartmouth's heritage of Puritan piety had faded; its rural isolation no longer seemed an asset; the school needed a fresh, up-to-date public image. This Hovey obligingly supplied in the rousingly successful "Men of Dartmouth":

> They have the still North in their hearts,
> The hill-winds in their veins,
> And the granite of New Hampshire
> In their muscles and their brains.[1]

We may smile today at this chilly, rockbound portrait, so naïvely and unconsciously anti-intellectual. Yet it exactly suited the emerging, collegiate spirit of the day. Hovey's song not only subordinated mind to muscle; it also associated both of these with the ruggedness of nature rather than the refinements of culture. In doing so, it turned the disadvantage of Dartmouth's location into an asset: it suggested to the men of Dartmouth their particular claim to the virility that college men throughout the country eagerly desired.

A rage for competitive athletics and for out-of-doors activities of all kinds was sweeping the campuses of the nation. A combative team spirit became virtually synonymous with college spirit; and athletic prowess became a major determinant of institutional status. Football made the greatest impact. Sedulously cultivated by Yale in the 1880's, it expanded into a big business after Walter Camp in 1889 named the first All-American team. But football dominated only the autumn; other seasons required their appropriate rites. Older sports such as baseball and track flourished in the spring. To fill the winter gap and to arrest the flight of students from the confines of the gymnasium, a YMCA teacher invented basketball in 1891. It was taken up almost at once. Intercollegiate wrestling matches soon followed.[2] Dartmouth, following Hovey's lead, learned to feature skiing and winter carnivals.

The transformation of the colleges into theaters of organized physical combat deserves our attention because it illustrates the master impulse that seized the American people in the 1890's and reshaped their history in the ensuing decades. Theodore Roosevelt articulated that impulse in a famous speech delivered in 1899, "The Strenuous Life." Denouncing "the soft spirit of the cloistered life" and "the base spirit of gain," Roosevelt told his listeners to "boldly face the life of strife . . . for it is only through strife, through hard and dangerous endeavor, that we shall ultimately win the goal of true national greatness."[3] If these words struck the keynote of Roosevelt's own career, they also sounded the tocsin of a new era. Countless others, in their various ways, expressed similar feelings. John Jay Chapman, a leading cultural critic, flayed the tepid conformity, the pervasive desire to please, the shuffling and circumspection, the "lack of passion in the American." Even Henry James—surely as inhibited and cerebral a novelist as America has produced—put into the mouths of his emotionally starved protagonists a choked cry for vivifying experience. "Don't forget that you're young," Strether tells little Bilham in *The Ambassadors*. "Live all you can; it's a mistake not

THE REORIENTATION OF AMERICAN CULTURE IN THE 1890'S

to. It doesn't so much matter what you do in particular, so long as you have your life."[4] Common folk felt much the same way. From their scorn of frailty and evasion, Americans minted a whole range of new epithets, which gained currency in the 1890's: sissy, pussyfoot, cold feet, stuffed shirt.[5]

From the middle of the nineteenth century until about 1890 Americans on the whole had submitted docilely enough to the gathering restrictions of a highly industrialized society. They learned to live in cities, to sit in rooms cluttered with bric-a-brac, to limit the size of their families, to accept the authority of professional elites, to mask their aggressions behind a thickening façade of gentility, and to comfort themselves with a faith in automatic material progress. Above all, Americans learned to conform to the discipline of machinery. The time clock, introduced into offices and factories in the early 1890's, signaled an advanced stage in the mechanization of life.[6]

By that time a profound spiritual reaction was developing. It took many forms, but it was everywhere a hunger to break out of the frustrations, the routine, and the sheer dullness of an urban-industrial culture. It was everywhere an urge to be young, masculine, and adventurous. In the 1890's the new, activist mood was only beginning to challenge the restraint and decorum of the "Gilded Age." Only after 1897, when the oppressive weight of a long, grim economic depression lifted, did a demand for vivid and masterful experience dominate American politics. Yet the dynamism that characterized the whole political and social scene from the turn of the century through World War I emerged during the 1890's in large areas of popular culture. To some of these areas historians have not yet paid enough attention to appreciate the extent and nature of the change that was occurring. We are well aware of the aggressive nationalism that sprang up after 1890. We do not so often notice analogous ferments in other spheres: a boom in sports and recreation; a revitalized interest in untamed nature; a quickening of popular music; an unsettling of the condition of women.

The sports revolution in the colleges was part of a much broader upsurge of enthusiasm for outdoor recreation and physical culture in the American public at large. The growing zest for both spectator and participant sports amazed contemporary observers in the early nineties. The most universal sport was bicycling, one of the great crazes of the decade. Primarily social and recreational rather than a means of necessary transportation, bicycles reached a total of one million in 1893 and ten million in 1900. Bicycle clubs and championship races excited enormous interest. Among games, baseball retained its primacy at both the professional and sandlot levels.[7] It did not, however, enjoy the sensational growth of other sports that catered more directly to a taste for speed or a taste for violence. Racing of various kinds, to say nothing of basketball, satisfied one; football and boxing fulfilled the other. Only boxing, among the spectacles of the nineties, grew as rapidly as football in public appeal. Most states of the union still outlawed professional prize-fighting as a relic of barbarism. Nevertheless, it began to lose its unsavory reputation after 1892, when padded gloves replaced bare fists and "Gentleman Jim" Corbett displayed an artful technique in defeating John L. Sullivan.[8] Henceforth heavyweight champions loomed large among American folk heroes.

An accompanying gospel of health through rugged exercise spread literally by leaps and bounds. Of the many shamans who arose to lead the cult, Bernarr Macfadden was the most successful. His career began at the World's Fair in Chicago in 1893, where he demonstrated the muscular attractions of an exerciser. He advanced through health clubs and lectures and won a national audience as publisher of the magazine *Physical Culture*. The first issue, appearing in 1899, flaunted his slogan: "Weakness Is a Crime."[9]

Closely linked with the boom in sports and health came an enthusiasm for the tonic freshness and openness of nature. This too had both a participant and a spectatorial aspect. At its mildest, participation meant escaping to the country astride a bicycle, taking up the newly imported game of golf, or going to the innumerable vacation resorts that emphasized their outdoor facilities. Somewhat more strenuously, it meant hiking and camping. In 1889 nature-lovers launched a campaign in behalf of California's redwood forests, and Congress in the following year created Yosemite, Sequoia, and General Grant National Parks. During the ensuing decade hundreds of nature-study clubs formed to encourage amateur naturalists. At least fifty-two periodicals devoted to wild life began publication.[10] In fact, the flood of nature writing, based on intimate knowledge and vivid observation, registered a major shift in popular interests. Only the leading novelists exceeded the popularity of some of the nature writers, such as John Muir and Ernest Thompson Seton, whose first books appeared in 1894 and 1898 respectively.[11]

Although the outdoors movement clearly drew upon a traditional American distrust of the city, it also ministered to the more general psychological discontents of the 1890's. Among the values that middle-class Americans were rediscovering in nature, two stand out. For one, the great outdoors signified spaciousness—an imaginative release from the institutional restraints and confinements Americans had accepted since the Civil War. It is suggestive that one of the most prominent features of the return to nature was a veritable craze for bird-watching. In a six-year-period New York and Boston publishers sold more than 70,000 textbooks on birds, while a children's magazine, *Birds,* reached a circulation of 40,000 in its first year of publication.[12] Congress had chosen a great soaring bird as the national emblem over a century before, and a bird on the wing continued to symbolize for Americans the boundless space they wished to inhabit.

Secondly, nature meant—as Hovey's description of Dartmouth men indicated—virility. It represented that masculine hardiness and power that suddenly seemed an absolutely indispensable remedy for the artificiality and effeteness of late nineteenth-century life. Nothing revealed the craving for nature's untamed strength so well as the best-selling fiction of the late nineties. For decades the popular novel had concentrated on domestic or rococo subjects rather than wilderness adventures. Above the level of the dime novel, the wild West had played very little part in fiction since the 1850's. Now it came back with a rush in a best-selling Canadian thriller, Ralph Connor's *Black Rock* (1898), in Jack London's red-blooded stories of the Klondike, and in Owen Wister's classic cowboy tale, *The Virginian* (1902). In effect, these and other writers were answering James Lane Allen's plea of 1897 for a reassertion of the masculine principle of virility and instinctive action in a literature too much dominated by the feminine principle of refinement and delicacy.[13]

A similarly muscular spirit invaded popular verse and music. The conventional style of song in the late nineteenth century was mournful and nostalgic. The fascination with death in such poems as Eugene Field's "Little Boy Blue," and with parting in such hit tunes as "After the Ball," betrayed a loss of youthfulness of American culture. Against this drowsy mood, a new generation of highspirited poets and musicians affirmed the masculine principle. Richard Hovey, who aspired to higher things, won a great popular success as co-author of *Songs from Vagabondia* (1894), which perfectly expressed the fresh out-of-doors spirit. Like no poems since Whitman's, these combined the love of nature, the freedom of the open road, the rollicking comradeship of men, and the tang of vivid experience.[14]

Meanwhile, cheerful energetic tunes spread from the midways and the outdoors amusement parks that were themselves symptoms of a new era. "Ta-ra-ra-boom-der-e," first published in 1891, struck a new, rhythmically vital note. Thereafter itinerant Negro pianists taught the white public the excitement of ragtime, a form of syncopation applied against a steady bass rhythm. A high-kicking dance step called the cakewalk spread along with the ragtime craze. In vain, custodians of respectablity denounced this "nigger music" and the "vulgar," "filthy" prancing that went with it.[15]

Both the new music and the new athleticism contributed to

the emergence of the New Woman. Her salient traits were boldness and radiant vigor. She shed the Victorian languor that had turned American middle-class society—as William Dean Howells noted in 1872—into a hospital for invalid females. Women took to the open road in tremendous numbers on bicycles suitably altered by an American inventor. They sat for portraits clutching tennis rackets; they might be seen at the new golf clubs or at the race tracks smoking cigarettes. In 1901 they could learn from Bernarr Macfadden's book, *The Power and Beauty of Superb Womanhood*, that vigorous exercise "will enable a woman to develop in every instance muscular strength almost to an equal degree with man."[16]

> Running, jumping, and natation, navigation, ambulation—
> So she seeks for recreation in a whirl.
> She's a highly energetic, undissuadable, magnetic,
> Peripatetic, athletic kind of girl![17]

The New Woman was masculine also in her demand for political power. The women's suffrage movement had been crotchety and unpopular; now it blossomed into a great nation-wide middle-class force. Significantly, its only state-wide victories prior to 1910 were won in the wide open spaces of the Rocky Mountain West.[18]

While women became more manly, men became more martial. By 1890 the sorrow and weariness left by the Civil War had passed; jingoism and a deliberate cultivation of the military virtues ensued. The United States picked quarrels with Italy, Chile, and Great Britain before it found a satisfactory target in the liberation of Cuba. A steady build-up of naval power accompanied these crises. One interesting feature of the rising respect for military prowess was an extraordinary cult of Napoleon. The first two instalments of Ida Tarbell's biography of Napoleon in *McClure's Magazine* doubled its paid circulation; and hers was only one of twenty-eight books about the Corsican general published in the United States in the three years from 1894 to 1896. For a collective symbol of the strenuous life, myth-makers depended heavily on the Anglo-Saxon race, which they endowed with unprecedented ferocity. A Kansas senator, for example, proudly described his race as "the most arrogant and rapacious, the most exclusive and indomitable in history."[19]

Meanwhile flag ceremonies, such as the newly-contrived pledge of allegiance, entered the school houses of the land. Patriotic societies multiplied as never before. In function they resembled the cheer leaders who were becoming so prominent a part of the big football spectacles, and who lifted the massed ranks of students into a collective glory. The link between the new athleticism and the new jingoism was especially evident in the yellow press: William Randolph Hearst's *New York Journal* created the modern sports page in 1896, just when its front page filled with atrocity stories of the bloody debauchery of Spanish brutes in Cuba.[20] At the same time the new music produced such martial airs as John Philip Sousa's masterpiece of patriotic fervor, "Stars and Stripes Forever" (1897), and "A Hot Time in the Old Town" (1896), which Theodore Roosevelt adopted as the official song of his Rough Riders. Indeed, Roosevelt was the outstanding fugleman of the whole gladiatorial spirit. He loved the great outdoors, the challenge of sports, the zest of political combat, the danger of war. He exhorted women to greater fecundity. He brought boxing into the White House and contributed immensely to its respectability.[21]

The change in temper I have been describing did not occur in the United States alone. It swept over much of western Europe about the same time. Its most obvious manifestations appeared in the navalism and jingoism of the time: the various national defense societies, the Pan-German League, the bombast of Wilhelm II, the sensational journalism of the Harmsworth brothers, the emotions that swirled around General Boulanger and Captain Dreyfus. Europe was perhaps more receptive than America to the militaristic aspects of the new mood. Two Englishmen, H. Rider Haggard and Rudyard Kipling, popularized the martial and masculine adventure story before respectable American authors turned to that genre. In other respects, however, America may have some claim to priority and leadership. The outdoors movement may have started in America, although England and Germany were not far behind.[22] The New Woman, together with her bicycle, materialized in England and in America about the same time; but the achievement of political rights and economic independence came more easily in this country than anywhere in Europe. The very phrase "New Woman" may have originated in the talk of an American character in an English novel that had its greatest success in the United States. Sarah Grand's *The Heavenly Twins*, published in 1893, expounded feminist ideas in a glamorous setting and sold five times as many copies in America as in England.[23]

In the sports revival, which also affected both continents, Americans seized a commanding lead. No people except the British loved athletic contests so much; and the Americans clearly excelled in ferocity. They won most of the events in the early Olympic Games, nine out of fourteen at Athens in 1896 and fourteen out of twenty at Paris in 1900. They racked up a disproportionate number of "world records."[24] They so dominated professional boxing that the championship of the United States became, from 1892 onward, identical with that of the world. A French observer, bemused by the American taste for pugilism, concluded that it was "too brutal a sight for a Frenchman of the nineteenth century."[25]

On the other hand, Europeans were intoxicated by the energy of American music. "Ta-ra-ra-boom-der-e" spread through Britain and beyond like an epidemic. "No other song ever took a people in quite the same way," an English historian tells us. "It would seem to have been the absurd *ça ira* of a generation bent upon kicking over the traces."[26] Translated into French as *"Tha-mara-buom-di-hé,"* the song proved a great hit in the leading Parisian cabarets. Across the Atlantic also went the cake walk, dazzling the music halls of London and Paris, and Sousa's band, giving Europe its first taste of ragtime.[27] The taste suited. In 1908 Claude Debussy used this American idiom for *The Golliwog's Cakewalk*.

The United States was not merely involved in the newly aggressive and exuberant mood of Europe; it was one of the instigators.

Can as much be said about American high culture during the same period? Were American art, literature, philosophy, and social thought undergoing an awakening comparable to the upheaval in popular feelings? Were American intellectuals significantly involved in the psychic turbulence so widespread in Western civilization? I believe they were. On both continents the sensitive as well as the vulgar felt the quickening call to strenuous experience. Although trans-Atlantic communication of ideas was intermittent and usually sluggish, a common cultural crisis in the 1890's affected intellectuals throughout the Western World.

This crisis followed upon the dominion that a materialistic outlook had won during the immediately preceding decades. From the 1860's through the 1880's, in Europe and America alike, the combined prestige of science and business enterprise shaped the direction of thought. During these years romantic idealism declined. So did religious vitality in the face of a sweeping secularization of values. Ornateness and a certain heaviness of style prevailed. All encompassing, monistic systems of thought were in favor: Spencerian and Hegelian systems contended in America; Comtean positivism and Marxian socialism loomed large in Europe. A triumphant belief in evolutionary progress, although much stronger in America than in Europe, everywhere blunted moral sensitivity.

By 1890 this vesture of assurance and complacency was wearing through. If failed to cover the emotional and material needs of the laboring classes; it did not entirely smother the conscience of the middle class; and it was too tight a fit for many intellectuals. For the latter, the cult of progress, stability, and materialism was becoming oppressive and suffocating. It brought restraint and uniformity into the world of thought without resolving the increasing conflicts in society.

The first response of intellectuals to the obvious social dislocations of an urban, industrial age was an attempt to strengthen the framework of order and to reinterpret the path of progress. The equipment of liberalism with a collective social ethic constituted the principal achievement of social thought both in England and in America in the 1880's—a work accomplished in one by Thomas Hill Green and the Fabians, and in the other by Henry George, Lester F. Ward, William Dean Howells, and a variety of historical economists. But these ideas made only modest headway in the following decade, while the problems they addressed grew much more acute. The special significance of the 1890's lay in a change of mood that swept many intellectuals beyond the earnest sobriety of the seventies and eighties. A readjustment of rational principles in the light of existing facts seemed in itself ineffective and uninteresting.

Two other strategies were possible; and the clash between them pervaded intellectual life. One might, in contempt or despair, spurn the trust in progress and find solace in contemplating the decline of a moribund civilization. Or one might look beyond the conventional framework of thought for access to fresh sources of energy. The first alternative was the counsel of defeat, whereas the second was a call to liberation. One way led to pessimism, decadence, and withdrawal into art for art's sake. The other pointed to a heightened activity and an exuberant sense of power. Both alternatives broke sharply with the complacent faith in material progress and human rationality that had ruled the Western world for two generations. Both the pessimists and the activists of the 1890's felt that the rational schemata of their time had become closed systems, imprisoning the human spirit. Pessimists accepted the denial of responsibility and purpose. Activists, on the other hand, attacked closed systems and created meanings from the flux of experience.

The acid of defeat and the elixir of liberation mingled in the intellectual ferment of the decade. A good many Americans as well as Europeans tasted both, with lasting effect. In general, however, one may say that the elixir proved an effective antidote to the acid. The strenuous spirit so prominent in popular culture quite generally overcame a defeatist spirit among intellectuals. The melancholy of the *fin-de-siècle* belied its name: it lifted before the end of the century.

This was especially the case in the United States, where a pessimistic outlook had only recently taken root in a serious way. Worldly pessimism comprised an important strain in European thought since the Enlightenment. Americans, however, had derived their sense of evil from the bracing doctrines of Calvinism, and they encountered the world with determination to resist it. Neither the terrors of personal frustration as in Poe nor the transcendental doubts of Melville had resulted in a pessimistic philosophy of life. The emergence of such an outlook was therefore a milestone in American intellectual history.

The melancholy and the ennui that invaded certain fastidious American minds in the late eighties and early nineties bore the direct imprint of European decadence. Schopenhauer together with Spinoza and Lucretius provided the basic philosophical structure for most of the poetry that George Santayana wrote in the nineties; Leopardi, Swinburne, and the English aesthetes supplied additional models for the circle of Harvard poets that formed around Santayana in those years. In New York Edgar Saltus, who also began from Schopenhauer, published delicately scandalous novels resembling those of Oscar Wilde in their knowing insolence and perverse wit. Others were reading Ernest Renan appreciatively. Renan instructed Henry Adams in the artistic uses of a spiritually exhausted religion, as Adams drifted from the South Seas to the cathedrals of France.[28] The same lesson reached a wide public through Harold Frederic's best-selling novel, *The Damnation of Theron Ware* (1896). Here an ultra-civilized, skeptical Catholic priest reveals to a simple-minded Methodist clergyman the world-weary elegance of a religion of art. "The truth is always relative, Mr. Ware," Father Forbes concludes.[29]

Other writers, untouched by European aestheticism, arrived at a grimmer sort of pessimism. There was, for example, the savage irony of the San Francisco journalist, Ambrose Bierce, whose first book of short stories, *Tales of Soldiers and Civilians* (1891), depicted a pointless, mocking destiny. There was Henry Adams' brother, Brooks, whose *Law of Civilization and Decay* (1895) diagnosed the decline of Western civilization since the defeat of Napoleon and its impending dissolution. This powerful, serious book was perhaps the first modern formulation of a cyclical theory of history. It was certainly the first full length American critique of the conception of history as progress. More informally, Mark Twain was reaching the same conclusion. His laughter turned increasingly into bitterness, visions of destruction welled up at the end of *The Connecticut Yankee* (1889), and by the late nineties an explicit fatalism convinced Twain that history was an endless cycle of cruelty and corruption, "a barren and meaningless process."[30] E. L. Godkin too was giving up hope for the future of American civilization. The toughest minded of all of the nation's social philosophers, William Graham Sumner, was warning his fellow countrymen that the utmost they could do was "to note and record their course as they are carried along" in the great stream of time.[31]

Such attitudes exemplified the naturalistic determinism that originated with Darwin and Spencer and became increasingly oppressive as the century waned. Until the 1890's American intellectuals had tempered the naturalistic creed with a supreme confidence in their own destiny. In Europe evolutionary thought slipped more easily into a dark vision of a blind and purposeless universe. Thus the naturalistic novel, in which man appears as the hapless plaything of great impersonal forces, was well established in France and England before Stephen Crane in 1893 published *Maggie,* the first American example of the genre. Pessimism seems to have invaded American minds only after the actual course of social change clearly refuted the liberating significance Americans had imputed to the evolutionary process. By 1890 the consolidation of big organizations, the massing of population, and the growing intensity of class conflict were inescapably apparent.

These trends did not at all correspond to the individualizing movement that Herbert Spencer had confidently envisioned. Instead of an inevitable development from an "incoherent homogeneity to a definite, coherent heterogeneity," Brooks Adams observed a steady centralization and a loss of vital energy, which would result in anarchy. Henry refined the theory into one of a general degradation and dispersion of energy.[32] Many felt an erosion of their own independent station in society. Clearly, the survival of the fittest was not synonymous, as Darwinians formerly supposed, with the survival of the best. Nor did the course of events conform to the ancient belief in America's uniqueness, confidence in which had always provided an ultimate bulwark of the national faith in progress. "We are the first Americans," Woodrow Wilson gravely warned, "to entertain any serious doubts about the superiority of our own institutions as compared with the systems of Europe."[33]

A signal indication of the intensity of concern over these defeatist attitudes was the feverish discussion provoked by Max Nordau's book, *Degeneration*. I believe that no other European book of any kind published during the entire decade aroused so much comment in the American press. Even before its translation into English in 1895, the book received a long review in *The Critic*.[34] Soon the Sunday supplements and the daily papers were trumpeting its charges. Much of this attention resulted from the sheer sensationalism of Nordau's argument that the eminent artists and writers of the day were suffering from mental deterioration. Many, perhaps most, commentators regarded Nordau as at least as degenerate as the people he attacked. But his fundamental charge that the age was suffering from "a compound of feverish restlessness and blunted discouragement, of . . . vague qualms of a Dusk of Nations" touched a sensitive nerve.

When all this is said, the fact remains that pessimism became in America neither general nor profound. Sourness and irony Americans could sometimes stomach; they had little taste for despair. Even Henry Adams never ceased to struggle against despair, and Santayana transmuted it into a flawless serenity. Most

THE REORIENTATION OF AMERICAN CULTURE IN THE 1890's

American intellectuals resisted pessimism. Philosophers (with the partial exception of Santayana) rallied against it; literary critics denounced it; social scientists were challenged rather than overcome by it. Accordingly, the voices of negation rose from rather special quarters: from people who were being left behind. The most somber temperaments belonged, on the one hand, to old men like Twain and Sumner, who had fought the good fight through the seventies and eighties and who now lost heart; or they belonged, on the other hand, to men of patrician background like Adams, Saltus, and the Harvard poets, scions of old and cultivated families who felt displaced in a pushing, competitive, bourgeois world.

The naturalistic novelists cannot be included among either the old men or the patricians. They were young, and they came from middle-class homes. But it requires no close inspection to discover that Norris, Crane, London, and even Dreiser were only partly fatalistic. Unlike many European naturalists, they expressed the affirmative as well as the negative possibilities of their age. The American naturalists gloried in identifying themselves with the triumphant strength of nature or with the struggles of embattled man. Instead of observing life clinically, they celebrated power. "The world," intoned Frank Norris, "wants men, great, strong, harsh, brutal men—men with purpose who let nothing, nothing, nothing stand in their way."[35] Dreiser and London shared Norris's fascination with the ruthless pursuit of success. Crane spent his volatile life imagining and seeking war. Here, as Van Wyck Brooks has pointed out, began the cave-man tendency in modern American literature.[36] In the fierce joy of conflict these writers discovered the activist reply to the specter of an indifferent universe.

No one better reveals the instability of the pessimism of the nineties than its most systematic exponent, Brooks Adams. Younger and less cosmopolitan than his brother Henry, who remained generally defeatist, Brooks underwent a great conversion around 1898. He decided that the Spanish-American

War disproved his theory of history. Evidently centralization was leading not to a degradation but to a revival of national energy. Only Europe, not America, is decaying, Brooks chortled. "I am for the new world—the new America, the new empire . . . we are the people of destiny."[37] And he became henceforth an activist, who bombarded his fellow countrymen with advice on geopolitical strategy and public administration.

Thus Brooks Adams illustrates two of the spheres in which the strenuous life came to intellectual fruition. The escape from pessimism flung him into reform as well as imperialism; and since imperialism proved after a short while an unattractive outlet for American effort, his attention turned increasingly in the early twentieth century to the uses of power in domestic affairs. This happened to a great many American intellectuals. We know that imperialism and progressivism were closely related crusades, and it seems clear that together they largely banished gloom and anxiety in favor of an optimistic, adventurous engagement in social change.[38] The activism of the nineties contributed, therefore, to the hearty interest that progressive intellectuals showed in *doing* things, in closing with immediate practical realities, in concentrating on techniques rather than sweeping theories. The early twentieth century was not a very congenial period in America for the speculative thinker with interests remote from the facts of contemporary life. It was a time of administrative energy and functional thought.

Must we then conclude that the new activism had no constructive impact on other areas of thought, beyond concrete social issues? Did the clamorus vitality generated in the nineties exhaust itself in emotional kicks on one hand and in techniques of social reform on the other? Were its positive achievements only visceral and practical? Or did the shattering of closed systems and the relief of pessimism also enlarge the imaginative resources of American intellectuals? These questions do not admit of any final answer. But a brief comparison of three major intellectuals who participated in the cultural revolution of the 1890's may suggest how stimulating it could be in very diverse fields.[39]

THE REORIENTATION OF AMERICAN CULTURE IN THE 1890'S

William James was neither the first of the American pragmatists nor in every respect the greatest, but he was surely the most passionately concerned with emancipating his fellow men from tradition, apathy, and routine. His predecessor Charles S. Peirce was preoccupied with traditional metaphysical and logical problems, his successor John Dewey with gaining rational control of experience. James, standing between them, was the arch-foe of all intellectual systems, less concerned with organizing thought or experience than with validating their manifold possibilities. Although each of the major pragmatists took part in the intellectual life of the 1890's, James belongs to that decade in a very special sense. Having anticipated much earlier its revolt against pessimism and fatalism, James applied himself intensively to its spiritual needs. His *Principles of Psychology* came out in 1890. Thereafter he grew beyond his first career as a psychologist, greatly enlarged his interests and sympathies, and launched pragmatism as a broad philosophical movement.

For James the nineties were years of fulfilment and fame. For two young men born in the 1860's—Frederick Jackson Turner and Frank Lloyd Wright—this was the crucially formative period, when the emancipation that James preached was taking effect. Turner received his Ph.D. at Johns Hopkins in 1890 and returned to Wisconsin to work out his own ideas about American history. In the next few years all of his major ideas emerged. The famous address of 1893 on the significance of the frontier announced his revolt against the eastern, European-oriented view of American history that then prevailed. In other work of the mid-nineties, Turner inaugurated a broadly economic interpretation of American history in terms of sectional cleavages.[40] Wright, a budding Chicago architect, also declared independence in 1893 by quitting his beloved master, Louis Sullivan, and opening his own office. During the course of the decade Wright developed his own personal, flexible style in opposition both to Sullivan's sentimentality and to the conventions of the European architectural tradition. Unknown to one another, James, Turner, and Wright were the great leavening and liberating figures in their respective disciplines at the turn of the century.

None of them engaged in the crude, swaggering bombast so prevalent in the popular activism of the period. Indeed, James roundly attacked people like Theodore Roosevelt who were arousing "the aboriginal capacity for murderous excitement which lies sleeping" in every bosom, and he once coolly remarked of his friend Oliver Wendell Holmes, Jr., that "Mere excitement is an immature ideal, unworthy of the Supreme Court's official endorsement."[41] Nevertheless, James, Wright, and Turner were in their own ways hardy, fighting men, full of zest for new experience, in love with novelty and experiment, eager to adapt philosophy, architecture, and history to the ever-changing needs of the present hour. James himself struck the distinctive note of the 1890's by interpreting all ideas as plans for action and by exalting the will.

All three men possessed exuberant, optimistic, restless personalities. Their brimming energies threatened continually to overflow any imposed discipline, so much so in the cases of James and Turner that neither succeeded in finishing the big, systematic book he wished to write. Neither in his intellectual habits was at all methodical. "Turner bubbled it out," one of his students remembers,[42] and the same could equally have been said of James. Wright had the strongest personality of the three. He ran away from home, scorned all formal education, and built within himself an oracular self-confidence touched with arrogance.[43] Only Wright wore his hair long to flaunt his independence, but James and Turner also enjoyed a poetic flair and a lilting heart.

Intellectually, their deepest affinity arose from a common opposition to all closed and static patterns of order. James's repugnance for a "block universe" is well known. "All 'classic,' clean, cut and dried, 'noble,' fixed, 'eternal' *Weltanschauungen* seem to me to violate the character with which life concretely comes and the expression which it bears of being, or at least involving, a muddle and a struggle."[44] This resembles Wright's hatred of the stiff classical and Renaissance traditions in architecture. A dynamic flow—an image of continual becoming—pervades Wright's buildings, and runs equally through James's philosophy. Similarly, Turner's history spoke always of men on the move, venturing westward, breaking the cake of custom, ever engaged in struggle and contradiction. Turner rebelled against the dominant mode of historical scholarship, which emphasized the stability and continuity embodied in the formal structure of institutions. He presented history not as a logical unfolding of constitutions but as a continual flux of experience. In breaking up American history into a balanced interplay of opposing sections,[45] Turner accomplished what James's pluralism achieved in philosophy and what Wright's juxtaposition of advancing and receding planes realized in architecture.

The revolt of these men against intellectual rigidities closely paralleled the assault in popular culture upon a confined and circumscribed life. It is hardly a coincidence that Turner and Theodore Roosevelt made the frontiersman the heroic figure in American history just at the time when he was becoming the hero of best-selling novels. Nor is it happen-stance that Wright did away with interior doors and widened windows just at the time when Edward Bok, editor of the *Ladies Home Journal,* launched spectacularly successful campaigns to clear out the clutter from parlors and the ugly litter from cities.[46] Like so many other Americans, James, Wright, and Turner were reaching out into the open air.

All three quite literally and passionately loved the out-of-doors. James and Turner were never so happy as when they were camping in the wilderness, and Wright felt as keenly as they the moral strength to be derived from the earth. His prairie houses, stretching outward to embrace the land, attest his fidelity to his mother's injunction, "Keep close to the earth, boy: in that lies strength."[47] For each of these men, nature signified not just power but also the freedom of open space. By explaining American democracy as the product of "free land," Turner extracted a dimension of freedom from the realm of necessity; and this is what

Wright did in constructing "the new reality that is *space* instead of matter."[48] Meanwhile, in philosophy, James argued against a restrictive materialism by emphasizing the incompleteness of visible nature and by calling attention to those natural facts of religious experience that suggest a vaster realm of spiritual freedom.[49] In a sense, he too converted matter into space.

In part, the open-air activists of the nineties were harking back to the old American values affirmed by Walt Whitman, the poet who most rapturously identified himself with boundless space.[50] Wright adored Whitman. Turner quoted him. James, the most discriminating of the three, put his finger exactly on Whitman's spaciousness:

> Walt Whitman owes his importance in literature to the systematic expulsion from his writings of all contractile elements. The only sentiments he allowed himself to express were of the expansive order; and he expressed these in the first person, not as your mere monstrously conceited individual might so express them, but vicariously for all men, so that a passionate and mystic ontological emotion suffuses his words . . .[51]

Appropriately, Whitman's reputation was just then emerging powerfully from the distrustful and evasive gentility that obscured it earlier. His flowing lines supplied the largeness and virility that more and more Americans wanted in order to overcome the "contractile elements" in late nineteenth-century culture. A biography of Whitman, published in 1896 by the influential nature-writer John Burroughs, made this appeal explicit:

> Did one begin to see evil omen in this perpetual whittling away and sharpening and lightening of the American type,—grace without power, clearness without mass, intellect without character,—then take comfort from the volume and the rankness of Walt Whitman? Did one begin to fear that the decay of maternity and paternity in our older communities and the falling off in the native population presaged the drying up of the race in its very sources? Then welcome to the rank sexuality and to the athletic fatherhood and

motherhood celebrated by Whitman. Did our skepticism, our headiness, our worldliness, threaten to eat us up like cancer? Did our hardness, our irreligiousness, and our passion for the genteel point to a fugitive, superficial race? Was our literature threatened with the artistic degeneration,—running all to art and not at all to power? Were our communities invaded by a dry rot of culture? Were we fast becoming a delicate, indoor genteel race? Were our women sinking deeper and deeper into the "incredible sloughs of fashion and all kinds of dyspeptic depletion,"—the antidote for all these ills is in Walt Whitman.[52]

Evidently the new appreciation of Whitman, the anti-formalism of James, Wright, and Turner, and the various popular displays of a quasi-primitive vitality arose from a common rebellion against patterns of confinement in life and thought. Evidently also this rebellion sprang to a large extent from indigenous circumstances and energies; it does not appear to have received its primary inspiration from abroad. In fact, the new activism was accompanied by a revulsion against European cultural leadership, and the principal innovators were markedly anti-European in their social and moral attitudes. As a young man Wright refused a splendid opportunity to study architecture in Europe, all expenses paid. He felt, when he did so, that he was "only keeping faith" with America. James, oppressed by the weight of the past world in Europe, returned to the less tradition-laden atmosphere of Harvard exclaiming, "Better fifty years of Cambridge than a cycle of Cathay!"[53] Turner, who conceived of American history as a movement away from Europe, gave our past so native a hue that his successors for half a century treated it as a largely endogenous phenomenon. All of these men associated Europe with the constraint and decrepitude they abhorred. All of them associated America with the freshness and openness they sought to revive.

Nevertheless, their rebellion paralleled a similar change in European thought and feeling, as we have already noticed in respect to popular culture. In Europe as well as America the balance shifted from a constricting pessimism to a regenerating activism. There, too, the change may be described broadly as a reaction against the stifling atmosphere of bourgeois materialism. Yet the strategy of the rebellion in European high culture had certain distinctive characteristics that may help us to understand the American experience.

A crude way of putting the matter is to say that cultural discontent among European intellectuals was more drastic.[54] American intellectuals did not—any more than the American painters of the day—go in for strong colors. One cannot imagine among them a Vincent Van Gogh or a Georges Sorel. Hardly anyone in America directly and belligerently assailed conventional standards of morality. American intellectuals did not, like so many Europeans, feel profoundly alienated from their own society and culture. James, Wright, and Turner conceived of themselves as revitalizing values rooted in American life. Feeling that great reserves of energy lay all around them, they did not look so far afield as those Europeans who turned to primitive myth or to the international proletariat. Nor did they look so far beneath the surface as those Europeans who plunged into the depths of the private self.

Nothing seems more striking in comparative terms than the absence in the United States of the radical subjectivity that was entering European thought. In European literature the symbolists were creating an art of equivocality, distortion, and illusion. In philosophy the Bergsonian doctrine of intuition and the Nietzschean celebration of the Dionysian ego were beginning to be heard. In psychology Freud was probing the strange world of dreams. In history the leading German theoreticians were declaring their independence from scientific laws and insisting on the subjective basis of historical knowledge. In all these fields, European intellectuals were rending the fabric of external reality and discovering truth in the depths of subjective, personal experience. In America, on the other hand, literature remained predominantly realistic, philosophy empirical, psychology behavioral, history scientific. Yet on both continents intellectuals were seeking liberation from closed systems and formalistic abstractions.

The difference may be explained largely in terms of contrasting environments. America was a big country with a relatively fluid rather than a relatively stable society. Here the restless intellectual reached outward to the range, flux, and variety of life around him. In Europe he was more likely to reach inward to the intense and often mystical feelings within himself. Americans rebelled by extending the breadth of experience, Europeans by plumbing its depths. For Americans liberation meant permissiveness, maneuverability, multiplication of the individual's relationships with the world outside himself, Accordingly, James celebrated multiplicity and constructed an essentially eclectic philosophy. Wright swept away confining walls and opened up fluid space. Turner widened the breadth of history in order to interrelate political, social, economic, and geographical changes.

Unready for the heightened subjectivity of European thought, American intellectuals did not engage in the accompanying criticism of scientific ideas. In Europe objective reality lost some of its authority. Americans, however, resisted sharp segregation between various levels and types of thought: between facts and values, intellect and intuition, the scientific and the supra-scientific. "Something there is that doesn't love a wall," an American poet declared some years later; and the chief American philosophers—James, Dewey, and Peirce—wanted to do away with walls separating subjective values from objective facts. For Americans the external world retained a promise of ultimate goodness and harmony.

Consequently, the broad and various reaches of nature provided the expansive Americans of the 1890's not only with the vitality they sought but also with a spacious alternative to the European self-consciousness they shunned. A genteel literary critic of the 1890's offers us a final summation of the intellectual strategy that—for better or worse—prevailed:

... nothing breeds doubt and despair so quickly as a constant and feverish self-consciousness, with inability to look at life and the world apart from our own interests, emotions, and temperament. This is, in an exceptional degree, an epoch of morbid egoism, of exaggerated and excessive self-consciousness; an egoism which does not always breed vanity, but which confirms the tendency to measure everything by its value to us, and to decide every question on the basis of our personal relation to it. It is always unwise to generalize too broadly and freely about contemporary conditions, but there are many facts to bear out the statement that at no previous period in the history of the world have so many men and women been keenly and painfully self-conscious; never a time when it has been so difficult to look at things broadly and objectively. . . .

From this heated atmosphere and from these representations of disease, put forth as reproductions of normal life, we fly to Nature, and are led away from all thought of ourselves. We escape out of individual into universal life; we bathe in the healing waters of an illimitable ocean of vitality. . . . To drain into ourselves the rivulets of power which flow through Nature, art, and experience, we must hold ourselves open on all sides; we must empty ourselves of ourselves in order to make room for the truth and power which come to us through knowledge and action; we must lose our abnormal self-consciousness in rich and free relations with the universal life around us.[55]

In keeping with his own gentility, Hamilton Wright Mabie softened the outreaching strategy of American culture. For him and for many other Americans it meant escape. It was a flight from travail, from complexity, from the terrors of self-awareness. Yet the great restlessness that seized the nations of the West in the nineties did not, even in America, dissipate itself in dreams of natural harmony. The psychic turbulence unloosed at that time continued to beat upon us in the twentieth century, and it has gradually involved Americans as well as Europeans in a deeper confrontation of themselves.

The Concept of Nature

by Albert William Levi

      The intuitions of poets and the underpinnings of literary life reflect the perturbations of mind which are a consequence of revolutions and transformations in philosophic thought. In 1798 Wordsworth in the "Lines Composed A Few Miles Above Tintern Abbey" crystallized a view of nature which was not only an implicit attack upon the cosmology of the eighteenth century, but was an earnest of that proto-romanticism which was to govern the mind of Europe for the next forty years.

>   For I have learned
> To look on nature, not as in the hour
> Of thoughtless youth; but hearing oftentimes
> The still, sad music of humanity,
> Nor harsh nor grating, though of ample power
> To chasten and subdue. And I have felt
> A presence that disturbs me with the joy
> Of elevated thoughts; a sense sublime
> Of something far more deeply interfused,
> Whose dwelling is the light of setting suns,
> And the round ocean and the living air,
> And the blue sky, and in the mind of man:

> A motion and a spirit, that impels
> All thinking things, all objects of all thought,
> And rolls through all things. Therefore am I still
> A lover of the meadows and the woods,
> And mountains; and of all that we behold
> From this green earth; of all the mighty world
> Of eye, and ear,—both what they half create,
> And what perceive; well pleased to recognize
> In nature and the language of the sense
> The anchor of my purest thoughts, the nurse,
> The guide, the guardian of my heart, and soul
> Of all my moral being.[1]

Six decades later Edmond and Jules de Goncourt, writing in their *Journal* on July 1, 1856, "have learned to look on nature" in quite another fashion:

> Back from a day in the country, we dined this evening at La Terrasse, a cheap restaurant covered with chipped gilt trellis-work to which cling a dozen dried-up climbing vines, and we have across the way from us the sinking sun lighting up with its dying rays the shrill colors of the posters stuck up over the Panorama Arcade. Never, it seems to me, were my eye and heart more rejoiced than by the sight of this thick ugly plaster assailed by huge letters and scrawled over, dirtied, and smeared with the advertisements of Paris. Here everything is by man and belongs to man, except for an occasional sickly tree growing out of a crack in the asphalt, and these leprous house fronts speak to me as nature has never done. The generations of our time are too civilized, too old, too deeply enamored of the factitious and the artificial to be amused by the green of the earth and the blue of the sky. And here I shall make a strange confession: standing before the canvas of a good landscape painter, I feel myself more in the country than when I am in the middle of a field or wood.[2]

Not sixty years but a millenium separates the philosophies of nature which inform these two quotations. In Wordsworth we have a spirit which reminds us of the Virgilian attitude, the explorations of Chateaubriand, the paintings of Poussin and Constable, the moralized nature which is never far from the thoughts of Tolstoi's landed nobility. In the Goncourts we have something more reminiscent of Dostoievski's urban proletariat, Spengler's late city man, Utrillo's obsession with the leprous and peeling walls of Montmartre, the moribund megalopolitanism of the early Henry Miller. For Wordsworth "the light of setting suns" is the abode of a sublime sense of natural presence; for Edmond de Goncourt it is but a searchlight seeking out the scabrous advertisements of Paris.

But we have something here, I think, which reveals much more than the simple difference between 1798 and 1856, between the brilliant upsurge of the romantic passion for nature, and the prosaic artificiality of bourgeoise life which is the inevitable consequence of the industrial revolution. For Wordsworth nature is not the object of science, but a mystic unity, and since to view it thus is itself a "natural response" (and may possibly show a better realization of what nature is all about than a more precise physics), it indicates a phase of knowledge infinitely closer to "acquaintance" than to "description." For Wordsworth nature is wonderful, unfathomed, alive, the sanction of our morality and the source of our refreshment. And as Santayana says:

> The word nature is poetical enough: it suggests sufficiently the generative and controlling function, the endless vitality and changeful order of the world in which I live.
> Faith in nature restores in a comprehensive way that sense of the permanent which is dear to animal life. The world then becomes a home, and I can be a philosopher in it. . . .[3]

For Wordsworth too, the world of nature was a "home," and thus he too fancied himself a philosopher in it. And in what follows I want to take this *matrix version of nature* as a norm (this concept which implies "creativity" and "relatedness" and which alternatively uses the metaphors of a mother and her child or of the soil and the plant in which it is nourished[4] to illuminate the relationship of man to his natural environment), and to show (1) how it has fared in the philosophies of the contemporary world, and (2) how its contemporary fate is prefigured in the philosophic expressions of the European mentality during the years 1880-1900.

But before proceeding to either of these basic tasks, I should like to call attention to a profound dualism which underlies every treatment of nature—I mean the double origin of the concept and the dilemma with which it is in consequence confronted. For the idea of nature, as I have shown at length elsewhere,[5] is both the object of an exact science and a literary art; it belongs both to the most extreme efforts to formalize the structure of our experience and to project into it our deepest intuitions of feeling and emotion and value. In the works of Sir Isaac Newton nature is the elaborate construct of the scientific understanding in all its purity—that is to say, with every mythological, dramatic, and purposive element systematically expurgated. In Wordsworth (and even more particularly in Virgil) nature is the rich product of a teleological imagination—related to, but far more sophisticated than, primitive mythologizing—and retaining a view of the cosmos which finds it colorful, humanly exciting, highly dramatic, and deeply endowed with those qualities which assert its relationship to human purpose.

But this dualism of cultural response in our epistemic equipment which finds a polar relevance in the functioning of the human understanding on one side and the human imagination on the other is never unambiguously absolute and disjunctive in its appearances. No work of literary imagination exists which does not reflect a certain lure of scientific clarity and logical structure. No work of scientific understanding exists which has expurgated without residue the temptation toward myth-making and drama. It is in the service of resisting this curious temptation toward a mixture of modes that the respective vocabularies of "a scientific chain of meaning" and of "a humanistic complex" have been directed. Obviously, no such dichotomy has ever functioned with complete success, and the deepest problems in connection with a concept such as that of "nature" stem from the fact that it stands at the very point of intersection of these diverse linguistic strategies. For if works like Newton's *Philosophiae Naturalis Principia Mathematica* and Virgil's *Aeneid* (or Wordsworth's "Prelude," "Excursion," or "Tintern Abbey") constitute the extremes of this elaborate continuum, it is obvious that works like Plato's *Timaeus,* Lucretius' *De Rerum Natura*, Holbach's *Le Système de la nature*, and Whitehead's *Process and Reality* fall somewhere in between.

The implication of this unresolved dualism for what I have called "the matrix version of nature" is, I think, clear. For, while it has become almost *cliché* to distinguish between a mechanistic (Newtonian) and a romantic (Wordsworthian) conception of nature,[6] the degree to which the one has been infected by the presuppositions of the other has been somewhat neglected. Santayana's mythological materialism—a type of naturalism which owes even more to the imagination than it owes to science—with its basic metaphor of "the world as our home" is paralleled by the naturalism of Woodbridge—no longer as influential as it once was, but seeking somehow to reconcile the spirit of Aristotle with that of John Dewey. Like Darwin and Dewey, he holds that we begin our reflections as animals living in a visible world around us; like Aristotle, he understands by nature that which is in movement and in process, but he is also too much under the mythic spell to see in nature merely that which is exhausted by a calculus of measurability. And the consequence is that Woodbridge's nature is a "Nature"—a substantive spelled with a capital "N":

> In so naming it, I have no intention of conveying information about it. So I spell the name with a capital letter to indicate that it is what we call a "proper" and sometimes "Christian" name. The heathen had in their languages somewhat equivalent words, suggestive of generation and decay, and that suggestion still influences our English use of the Latin word *natura,* as if Nature were once born of dubious

parents and might later die, remaining meanwhile like a fertile mother, who, in spite of never having had a husband, has had a prodigious offspring. I confess to some sympathy with the heathen in this matter. Personification is difficult for me to resist. I am afflicted with a sense of indecency whenever I refer to Nature as "it." My ancestors are all dead, but I feel like a child of Nature, cradled in her arms until my turn comes to die and to remain somewhere and somehow in her embrace. This sentiment I shall not resist....[7]

The implication of such a conception is not merely animism. It implies that when one asks: "For whom is there Nature?" one answers not merely "for chemists and physicists and biologists," nor even "for primitives and poets," but also "for farmers and forest rangers, for space explorers and city-dwellers thinking of the summer vacation."

The naturalism of Woodbridge unobtrusively combines the animism of Wordsworth with the scientific seriousness of Newton, but in this respect it is hardly new. In fact it only repeats the curious mixture of the modes which is already discernible in Holbach. Holbach, like most of the French eighteenth century, lies under the spell of Newtonian rationalism—I mean the fact that nature is orderly, that it is patient of mathematical interpretation. But for one who stresses the system, the inevitability, the *mechanism* of nature, the conclusion to which Holbach comes as to the felicity which follows when one submits to the claims of the encompassing Mother, recalls the ambience of late Roman Stoicism, and the curious animism which always lies just under the surface in any doctrine of natural law. Holbach begins with a perfect paraphrase of the Newtonian world view:

> Men always deceive themselves when they abandon experience for the systems begotten by the imagination. Man is the work of nature. He exists in nature. He is subject to its laws. He cannot break away from them. . . . For a being formed by nature and circumscribed by her laws, there exists nothing beyond the great whole of which he forms a

part and whose influences he experiences. . . . The universe, that vast assemblage of everything that exists, only presents us with matter and motion; its totality shows us only one immense and uninterrupted chain of causes and effects. . . .[8]

But he ends with an apostrophe to man's debt to and reliance upon nature which in its gaudy rhetoric outdoes anything which is to be found in "Tintern Abbey" or "The Tables Turned":

> Listen then to nature, for she never contradicts herself. "Oh thou," she says, "who, following the impulse which I have given you in every instant of your life, seek for happiness, do not resist my sovereign law. . . . It is in my empire alone that freedom reigns. Tyranny and slavery are forever banished from it, and equity watches over the security of my subjects. They are maintained in their rights. Benevolence and humanity connects them in amicable bonds. . . . Return then, false child, return to nature. She will console you, will drive from your heart those fears that overwhelm you, these anxieties which oppress you, these hates which separate you from the humanity that you ought to love. Return to nature, to humanity, to yourself. . . ."[9]

I speak of some similarity between Wordsworth and Holbach. Forty years ago Professor Irving Babbitt was complaining about Wordsworth. Although it is asserted, he said, that there is a greater spiritual elevation in Wordworth's communings with nature than in those of Rousseau or Chateaubriand, his spirit does not really differ from theirs. In both, Babbitt thought, was to be found the same abdication of the intellectual and critical faculties. But Babbitt's dissatisfaction with the romantic response to nature shows him to be curiously related to the city-bred artificiality of the Goncourts. He cites Boileau with approval as an example of seventeenth century "humanism":

> Boileau says: "Let nature be your sole study." What he means by nature appears a few lines later: "Study the court and become familiar with the town."[10]

But of course to see nature only in the court and in the town is surely expressive of the same mentality which delights "in everything that is by man and belongs to man" and prefers the leprous house fronts of the capital city to the green of the earth and the blue of the sky. Nor is it fortuitous (as Spengler and Simmel have both pointed out) that this megalopolitanism should be associated with a poverty of feeling and affect, and with a conscious elevation of the values of the intellect. The passage previously quoted from the Goncourt *Journal* was for July 1, 1856. Sixteen days later they animadverted on the novel in a fashion which fits perfectly with the previously rendered comments on nature:

> After having read Poe, a revelation of something which criticism does not seem to have suspected. Poe—a new literature, the literature of the twentieth century; the scientific miracle, the creation of fable by a plus *b,* a literature at once monomaniacal and mathematical. Imagination the product of analysis; Zadig an examining magistrate; Cyrano de Bergerac the pupil of Arago. *Things* taking a greater role than *beings.* And love—already in the works of Balzac subordinate to money—love making way for other sources of interest. In a word—the novel of the future bound to make more of what happens in the brain of humanity than in its heart.[11]

The temper of the Goncourts' reflections is prophetic—whether they are predicting the dominance of intellect over feeling or sensing nature more in the canvas of the landscape painter than in the actual valley of the Loire—and I have referred to them in contrast to Wordsworth, because the reference makes, I think, an apt commentary upon the conditions of European mentality which are at the root of the fate which the concept of nature has suffered in the philosophic domain during the last hundred years. For that *matrix version of nature,* prefigured in Wordsworth and only intermittently revived (as in the naturalism of Woodbridge and Santayana) has, with practically a single exception, lost the emotional dynamic which was imparted to it by the romantic movement. And the consequence has been that our concept of nature in the philosophy of the immediate past has vacillated between a scientism which has found "nature" to be a dispensible entity, and a humanism which has managed to pretend that the situation of man in anguish and despair can be described in almost total isolation from his grounding in the natural order. To this paradoxical contemporary philosophical situation I should now like to turn.

In the second volume of her *Mémoires* Simone de Beauvoir tells us of the youthful Sartre: that he did not like to walk in the country, that he was "allergic to chlorophyll," that the green of the fields exhausted him, that the only way he could tolerate it was to forget it.[12] The detail is small, and yet it tells us much—not only that there is something in the personality of this existentialist infinitely closer to the point of view of the Goncourts than to that of Wordsworth, but that the rejection of the matrix version of nature is not simply an accident of temperament, but can grow into something intrinsic to a philosophic position.

From the very settings of Sartre's theater one could infer that he was allergic to chlorophyll—in the claustrophobic hell of *Huis-Clos,* in the airless southern room of *La Putain respectueuse,* in Hoederer's small, efficient office of *Les Mains sales,* and in the smothering, dusty attic of his last play *Les Séquestrés d'Altona.* But even in his first, *Les Mouches,* it is apparent also. For although the locations ape Greek openness—a public square in Argos and a mountain terrace—the spirit remains permanently enclosed. I first saw *Les Mouches* in a smokey café-theater in Vienna on a stage no larger than that of the *Théâtre de la Huchette,* and one sensed at once that this was absolutely right. To perform *Les Mouches* in the open countryside at Delphi or Epidaurus would be as paradoxical and as absurd as to put on *Oedipus Rex* with mask and cothurnus in the "Circle in the Square."

But we are not here merely in the realm of supposition. For what Sartre's theater implies, his first and finest novel *La Nausée* openly asserts. No more characteristically existentialist an emotion can be imagined than the anguish of Roquentin in the park of Boueville as he gazes with slow-growing horror at the roots of the chestnut tree.[13] Long before this he has had encounters with nature, but they too had been abstract and uncanny. Walking along the seashore, he says like all the others, "The sea is green," or, "That is a seagull," but the perception is abstract and without the unthinking attribution of reality which makes experience unremarkable and normal. Instead he thinks like an Aristotelian logician: "The sea belongs to the class of green objects," or, "Green is a quality which inheres in the sea," and the landscape, instead of the nourishing matrix of natural existence, becomes for him like painted scenery in a theater at which one stares, oblivious of the play. But when finally this very abstractness turns dramatically into its opposite, the result is equally unnatural. For now the sense of "existence" becomes overwhelming and palpable; not merely a logical predicate but a quality making things monstrous and horrible, and characterized by all of those nauseous images of rankness and viscosity with which the Sartrean imagination is obsessed.

The root of the chestnut tree in the park suddenly becomes a black knotty mass, entirely beastly, entirely frightening, a fragment only of that general "paste of things" *(la pâte même des choses)* into which the nauseous sense of existence has transformed the world. The chestnut tree presses against the eyeballs, black and swollen and looking like boiled leather. The fountain nearby fills the nostrils with a green putrid odor. The entire park has become "moduldy" and "bloated"—as if nature itself were something disgusting and obscene, a bruise or a secretion or an "oozing" which is at once cataleptic and horrible.

"The root of the chestnut tree" section of *La Nausée* is also what we might expect from a philosopher who is "allergic to chlorophyll," but it is, at the same time, far more than an individual aversion or a personal idiosyncracy. For it represents an existentialist position which has learned as much from Marx as from Kierkegaard—to whom the experience of alienation refers not merely to the separation of man from his God, or of the worker from the product of his labor, but also of the human animal from his natural environment. To find that natural objects are permeated with a sense of alien "existence," and that this makes them "mouldy" and "bloated," "oozing" and "obscene," implies a revaluation of the concept of nature which is far from the simple assumptions of the eighteenth century. Nature is now no longer, as with Wordsworth, the anchor of the purest thought, the guide and guardian of the heart, nor, as with Holbach, the consolation of our loneliness, the dissipator of all fear and anxiety, the purger of social hatreds; she has become an alien presence, disgusting in her manifestations, threatening in her implications, profoundly disquieting to the contemplative mind.

It is true that Roquentin is more than a little mad. It is true that the Sartrean view of nature in its positive presentation is extreme. But it is also the case that the existentialist rejection of nature is very real even if most characteristically expressed by neglect rather than by direct attack. And the situation is here faintly reminiscent of what Aristotle remarked about the course of Greek philosophy; that it was cosmological and concerned with natural processes in the pre-Socratics, but with Socrates it turned to ethics, politics, and the immediate concerns of Athenian civic life. Existentialism, too, is an urban phenomenon, learning to concentrate its attention not upon nature but upon man, and it has therefore never been as much at home by the Mediterranean and in the Alps as in the *caves* of St. Germain and the *Lokales* of Schwabing.

That thirst for subjectivity, already apparent in Kierkegaard, has determined the existentialist stance. So that in Sartre's famous chef d'oeuvre, *L'Etre et le néant,* for every page which deals with "being-in-itself" (an objective category which might well in other circumstances have led to the construction of a philosophy of nature) there are a hundred dealing with the self, solipsism, the body as a social category, concrete relations with others, the "look," and the like. But we arrive at the heart of the matter when we come to Sartre's extreme stand on the problem of freedom. For here we have a clue to that fateful bifurcation (itself a product of the eighteenth century) which the philosophy of Kant has bequeathed to the modern world. Kant distinguished between two worlds: a world of nature, a sensible world accessible through the understanding and the principle of causality which is its chief interpretive tool, and an intelligible world of moral agents, operating according to the necessities of practical reason and the principle of freedom. It would be departing far from the truth to assert that Sartre and the entire existentialist movement with him is Kantian in its inspiration, but it is a fact that the philosophical justification for the separation of man and nature lies in Kant, and that existentialism, almost without exception,[14] has rejected the objective problems of the philosophy of nature to concentrate upon the inner perplexities of the human self.

The other major figures follow. Heidegger's chief preoccupation is with human *Dasein* and with that *Sorge* and *Sein zum Tode* which are its characteristic expressions. Jaspers' major themes are communication between man and man, the freedom of man's self-existence *(Selbstsein als Freiheit)* and the inescapable situations *(Grenzsituationen)* of our human existence. Here nature is not so much denigrated as abandoned. And that alienation of the human individual from the immediacies of a surrounding and comforting nature which accompanies the artifices of megalopolitan existence has now given rise to an obsessive "humanism"—not in the Deweyite sense that it emphasizes the human foreground of a natural world never far from the incentives and springs of human action, but rather in the Sartrean sense of an "existence" doggedly subjective, eternally victim of the transforming and alien gaze of the "other" and of the malicious power struggles of the competitive human predicament.

Existentialism has been one of the two major thrusts of contemporary philosophy. Positivism has been the other. And if the first has neglected a philosophy of nature in originating a philosophy of man, the latter has no less paradoxically destroyed a philosophy of nature by producing a philosophy of science. Here the chief exhibits are the works of Reichenbach and Carnap and it is to them that I should now quite briefly like to turn.

A brief glance at Carnap's brilliant (but later repudiated) early work *Der logische Aufbau der Welt*[15] will give the whole show away. For if one turns to its *Sachregister* under the heading "*Natur*," one finds the following: "Nature, see physical world, perceptual world," "Law of nature, see causality," "Natural science, see physics." This says it in a nutshell. For positivism, laws of nature have somehow dropped out of the picture and only "causality" remains, the science of nature has turned into "physics," and nature itself has vanished into that jungle of pointer readings and differential equations which can now be labeled—"the physical world." Positivism, true to its nineteenth century heritage, has sacrificed the birthright of nature's qualitative immediacy for that mess of potage which it calls the symbolic reconstitution of the world.

I do not wish in any way to call into question the necessity and the value of physical science. Its predictive requirements call for just such a symbolic reconstitution of the world. But philosophy is not physical science nor need it devote itself exclusively to an analysis of the methods and the conclusions of a science of this kind. The point is simple, for the positivistic enterprise has been largely devoted to just such analysis, and in the process the more immediate aspects of nature have fallen by the wayside. But a "philosophy of science" is by no means necessarily a "philosophy of nature." What Plato attempted in the *Timaeus,* what Aristotle attempted in the *De Caelo,* the *De Generatione et Corruptione,* and the *Historia Animalium,* what Lucretius brought to such magnificent focus in Books I, II, and V of *De Rerum Natura* is obviously no part of the positivistic intention.

For this there are at least several reasons. For one, the rise of positivism itself has been associated with the dominance of mathematics and physical science, and up to very recently there has been a profound difference in the respective qualities and implications of a physical and a biological science. Partly this has been due to the inherent abstractness of physics, to the postulation of its explanatory entities in abstraction from the immediate givens of sensory experience, and to the relative simplicity with which its principles yield to mathematical formalization. Botany, zoology, and even geology have been at once less abstract, more dependent upon the methods of gross observation, and less patient of mathematical interpretation. And the consquence has been that for the latter, the relation of "science" to "nature" has seemed more intimate and more immediate. It is no accident that men like Linnaeus and Buffon in the eighteenth century, as well as those like Charles Darwin and Louis Agassiz in the nineteenth, were indistinguishably "scientists" and "naturalists." The picture of Linnaeus endlessly exploring the Swedish countryside, of Darwin collecting more and more specimens as the "Beagle" circumnavigates the globe, of Buffon lovingly cultivating his gardens as Louis XV's curator of the *Jardin des Plantes,* and of Louis Agassiz tramping the glaciated highlands of Scotland or the unbroken trails of Appalachia, is rather different from that of Einstein sitting, pad and pencil in hand, before his desk at the Institute for Advanced Study in Princeton, or of Dirac inscribing endless formulae in his cubicle in the University of Paris. These pictures also invite comparison with the contrast between the nature romanticism of Wordsworth and the urban indifference of the Goncourts.

There is another reason, too, why the positivistic philosophy of science is not a philosophy of nature. This is because, unlike the scientific philosophy of the age of Galileo, Newton, and Descartes, it is anti-metaphysical. The seventeenth century believed both that the principles of mathematics were a built-in feature of the human mind and an expression of the purpose and intentions of the divine agency. It believed also that the justification of induction required a real connectedness in nature, some form of actual physical necessity which linked the immediate item of experience both with the past from which it had sprung and with the future to which it would give rise. The future is, in fact, predictable from the past precisely because nature possesses an antecedent structure, and the ultimate justification of the principle of induction becomes simply the rational perception of the order of nature.

Modern positivism rejects the concept of an order of nature, and it does so, as I have shown elsewhere,[16] through arguments which are ultimately derived from Hume. Hume shifted the locus of his analysis from a necessary connection between things in the world to a metaphysically uninterpreted "constant conjunction" of ideas in the mind. For, although for Hume there is constant conjunction, there is no longer any necessary connection, because the former is a mere "habit" of belief, not a necessity imposed by nature's real connectedness. This strategy of Hume is the backbone of contemporary positivism, for in its philosophy of science it dreams both of "a logic without ontology" and of a "scientific method without metaphysical presuppositions." And in the end this is to *conventionalize* any supposedly basic structural traits of nature. Even so standard a belief as that in the principle of the uniformity of nature is either abandoned or assimilated in distinctly non-metaphysical terms. Carnap absorbs it into a definition of inductive probability. Reichenbach formulates it as a mere "rule of procedure." In either case the belief in the existence of a real and pervasive characteristic of nature has been lost.

Existentialism has neglected a philosophy of nature in concentrating on a philosophy of man. Positivism has rejected a philosophy of nature by producing a narrowly restricted philosophy of science. Has the concept of nature received then no adequate or central treatment in the modern world? I think that it has, and that this treatment is to be found primarily in the work of Alfred North Whitehead. I should therefore like briefly to suggest along what lines such a modern defense of the older and more metaphysical conception of nature has taken place.

Whitehead's earliest speculations about physics (in direct opposition to positivism) assumes the direct relationship between a philosophy of nature and a philosophy of science:

Again I will make a further simplification, and confine attention to the natural sciences, that is, to the sciences whose subject-matter is nature. By postulating a common subject-matter for this group of sciences a unifying philosophy of natural science has been thereby presupposed.

What do we mean by nature? We have to discuss the philosophy of natural science. Natural science is the science of nature. But—What is nature?

Nature is that which we observe in perception through the senses. . . .[17]

If the last sentence were all, the advance would not be great. Carnap, too, has equated nature with the perceptual world, but the obvious, almost commonplace assertion that "Natural science is the science of nature" restores the notion of a realistic substrate which the positivistic conventionalism has so badly compromised. But this is not all. For Whitehead's characteristic claim is the intrusion of "life" into "nature," the claim that the old materialistic picture presented by physical science simply will not do; that nature in its entirety and in its details behaves not like a mechanism, but like an organism. Newton, says Whitehead, was a great physicist. He built a remarkable system, but he left all the factors of the system in the position of detached facts without sufficient reason for their working together. "He thus illustrated a great philosophic truth, that a dead nature can give no reasons. All ultimate reasons are in terms of aim at value. A dead nature aims at nothing. It is the essence of life that it exists for its own sake, as the intrinsic reaping of value."[18] None of the principles of mechanistic materialism so beautifully illustrated in Newton's system (particles having simple location in space, external relations between particles, the concept of "nature at an instant") are congruent with the idea of *nature alive*. Whitehead maintains that since Descartes the sharp division between nature and life has poisoned all subsequent philosophy. On the contrary he says: "The doctrine that I am maintaining is that neither physical nature nor life can be understood unless we fuse them together as essential factors in the composition of 'really real' things whose interconnections and individual characters constitute the universe."[19]

Whence has Whitehead derived this courage to fuse together nature and life, to see that no occasion of experience is without its tincture of mind, its component of feeling? Surely not from that cluster of concepts from contemporary physics—the physical field, the physical vector, quanta, vibratory entities—upon which he has drawn so heavily. Nor from the philosophy of Plato, to which he has so generously acknowledged his debt, and to which, in his opinion, all of modern philosophy (his own included) is but a series of footnotes. The source here is unbelievably the poetry of Wordsworth, with which he was obsessed even in the early days when he was systematizing the axioms of projective geometry, and whose "Prelude" he would read as if it were the Bible, poring over the meaning of various passages by night.[20]

Whitehead's commerce with nature was immediate and precise, and he has registered it in that remarkable paper "England and the Narrow Seas" where he speaks so intimately of the dangerous waters just off the coast of Kent, the channel with its fog and its gales, its sunken reefs and treacherous headlands:

> These currents have formed shoals which run northward from the Straits of Dover to the mouth of the Thames. My earliest recollections are entwined with flash lights from the lightships on the Goodwin Sands. We could see them on winter evenings from our nursery windows at the top of the house. Sometimes during a fog the boom of a gun would be heard at slow intervals across the sea. It was a ship ashore on the Goodwin Sands. At other times we saw rockets rise mysteriously from the dark waters. It was the Gull lightship signalling a wreck. Next day we were taken down to the harbour, and there was the lifeboat decked with flags; during the night it had been out and had saved the crew of some vessel slowly sinking in the merciless quicksands.[21]

We find here not an abstract symbolic relationship with nature, but an intimacy re-inforced by the full concrete experience: childhood, the fog, the Goodwin Sands, the flash of gunpowder across the sea, and we are prepared to understand why Whitehead felt such enormous kinship with Wordsworth—why, in fact, the latter seemed to him to represent the whole revolt against the scientific abstractions of the eighteenth century. There is in *Science and the Modern World* a famous chapter (Chapter V: "The Romantic Reaction"). Ostensibly it is the dialectical aftermath of the somewhat technical chapter which has come before, but it is in fact a paean to the insight of Wordsworth:

> Wordsworth was passionately absorbed in nature. It has been said of Spinoza that he was drunk with God. It is equally true that Wordsworth was drunk with nature. But he was a thoughtful, well-read man, with philosophical interests, and sane even to the point of prosiness. In addition, he was a genius. . . .
>
> He alleges against science its absorption in abstractions. His consistent theme is that the important facts of nature elude the scientific method. It is important therefore to ask what Wordsworth found in nature that failed to receive expression in science. I ask this question in the interest of science itself. . . .
>
> It is the brooding presence of the hills which haunts him. His theme is nature *in solido,* that is to say, he dwells on that mysterious presence of surrounding things, which imposes itself on any separate element that we set up as an individual for its own sake. He always grasps the whole of nature as involved in the tonality of the particular instance. . . .[22]

Whitehead's purpose in citing Wordsworth is essentially philosophical. The point which he wishes to make is not about poetry, but about science—how "strained and paradoxical is the view of nature which modern science imposes on our thoughts," and how much in need of supplementation this view is by the additional insights which are generic to romantic poetry. Wordsworth's nature is a living whole in which each item prehends the rest. Shelley's nature is essentially a nature of organisms functioning with some elementary tinge of perceptual experience. Both Shelley and Wordsworth are witness to the discord between the aesthetic intuitions of mankind and a mechanistic view of nature; both strongly suggest that the discord arises from a misunderstanding.

The major thrust of Whitehead's philosophy is to repair this misunderstanding in the direction to which romantic poetry points—to see that nature evolves, that in the deepest sense she is our home, that new and more massive integrations of feeling are the aim of such realizations as she is able to achieve.

If, now generalizing, we seek to summarize the situation with respect to the concept of nature in contemporary philosophy, we are not merely in a position to adopt Whitehead's words about modern science, but in addition to enlarge their scope so as to cover the contribution of existentialism as well. "How strained and paradoxical," we may say, "is the view of nature both of a positivism which reduces it to its qualityless symbolic equivalent and an existentialism which, insisting upon man's ontological uniqueness and fearful that a philosophy of nature (following the Darwinian strategy) in finding nature to be continuous might by that very fact compromise man's ontological uniqueness, neglects it altogether." So that with the two most lively schools of contemporary philosophic thought neglectful or unbearably narrow, with the older naturalism of Dewey, Woodbridge, and Santayana moribund, and with only the Wordsworthian emphasis of a Whitehead to stress what I have earlier called "the matrix version of nature," it is far from histrionic or forced to speak of a contemporary crisis in the concept of nature. I now wish to ask: How did this situation arise? Perhaps more accurately: What in the intellectual situation of the end of the last century (in the characteristic thrusts of the philosophic transformation of the years 1880-1900) has prefigured this crisis of our day?

To put the question in this way is to expose the basic presuppositions of my theory of intellectual history and to make clear the strategy concerning the history of ideas which I have invoked in this paper. Perhaps the most general statement which can be made about the history of ideas is that it presents a seamless web, that it is governed by the principle of continuity. And this suggests not only that for the intellectual historian the device of historical periodization is essentially artificial, but that any treatment of a fixed span of historical time may be approached as pure present, as anticipated future, or as remembered past. The first means as *immediate object,* the second in terms of *conditions,* the third in terms of *consequences.* A dramatist like Georg Büchner may in *Dantons Tod* treat the French Revolution as pure qualitative immediacy. An historian like Michelet has no sense of what Renaissance, Reformation, eighteenth century mean in themselves since he judges them all by the ideals of the French Revolution. Whereas Thiers (to complete the picture) explains the revolution itself by the abuses of *l'ancien régime* and uses the errors committed by preceding monarchs and ministers as causal agencies.

My own method in this paper is the method of consequences, for although in the first section I have suggested certain conditions in terms of which subsequent problems in the interpretation of the concept of nature have arisen, in the second I have addressed myself to the crisis in the concept of nature which must be explained. Insofar as an analogous preceding situation constitutes an explanation, we must return to the last twenty years of the nineteenth century. And when we do so, we find an interesting parallelism indeed. Friedrich Nietzsche produced the great bulk of his work between 1880 (when *Menschliches, Allzumenschliches* appeared) and 1892 (when *Also sprach Zarathustra* was finally completed), and in the content and spirit of the Nietzschean enterprise we find the sources for Sartre and the existentialist abandonment of nature. Ernst Mach wrote his *Wissenschaft der Mechanik* in 1883 and his *Analyse der Empfindungen* in 1886, and in Mach is that same positivistic spirit which is later in Reichenbach and Carnap to turn the philosophy of nature into a philosophy of science. F. H. Bradley wrote his *Appearance and Reality* in 1893, and in a famous chapter of that book (Chapter XXII—"Nature") Bradley anticipates the solution of the problem of nature which Whitehead is later to provide in *Science and the Modern World* and above all in *Process and Reality.* Thus the contemporary dimensions of the problem of nature represented in the grouping Sartre—Carnap—Whitehead finds its nineteenth century correlate in the grouping Nietzsche—Mach—Bradley. This is the nerve of what I have to suggest about the transformation in philosophy between 1880 and 1900, and it is to the meaning of this second grouping that I should now like to turn.

There is a paradox in the case of Nietzsche for, unlike Sartre, he was neither allergic to chlorophyll nor alienated from the obscure grandeur of nature. On the contrary, in his personal life he sought its solace in his solitariness much in the spirit of Wordsworth, and in those instances where he dares to speak personally, there are traces of the sea at Nice and Genoa and of the snow-capped peaks of Sils-Maria and the upper Engadine. The fifth book of *Morgenröte* begins with an apostrophe to the sea:

> Here is the sea; here we can forget the city.... Before us lies the ocean pale and sparkling; it cannot speak. The sky plays its eternal mute evening game with the colors red, yellow, and green; it cannot speak. The tiny cliffs and rocks which go out into the sea as if each one is searching to find the loneliest spot; they cannot speak. Beautiful and terrible is this strange silence which suddenly overcomes us and makes the heart swell.[23]

But the moment is short-lived. The passage continues: "Oh the faithlessness of this dumb beauty! How well could it speak, and how wickedly too if it wished.... Yet I pity you, Nature—because you must be silent even if it is only your malice which binds your tongue...."

This is perhaps far from the obsession of Roquentin with the root of the chestnut tree and the mouldy and bloated park in which it grows—Nietzsche only speaks of nature as "silent" and "malicious," whereas for Sartre it is "putrid" and "oozing" and "frightening"—but the consequences in the end are very similar. For the retreat from nature in Sartre which is predicated upon its intrinsic repulsiveness is prefigured in Nietzsche by a retreat before its icy unconcern. Up to the present, says Nietzsche, errors have been the power most fruitful in consolation; how could we expect the same from accepted truths? What have these truths in common with the sick condition of a suffering and degenerate humanity? If one is convinced (as was an earlier theological age) that man is the ultimate end of nature, then all natural knowledge must itself be useful and beneficial to man. But an age which has lost this conviction can perhaps take no real joy in natural science, but must rather reproach it for its "coldness, dryness, and inhumanity."

How differently, says Nietzsche, must the Greeks have viewed their "nature" when one reflects that in their eyes the same colors by which they represented human beings predominated in nature, and perhaps enabled them to conceive all natural phenomena as gods and demi-gods, that is to say, in human form.[24] But conversely, when the feeling exists that nature is ugly, wild, and tedious and that science is the enterprise which describes it, then philosophy arises (like rococo horticulture) to embellish it nearer the heart's desire and infuse into it as much "irrationalty" and "dreaminess" as will enable us to think of it once more as our home. Nietzsche, it is clear, is not a partisan of the matrix version of nature. For his objectivity leads him in the direction of a "descriptive" rather than an "interpretive" preference. Just so, he says characteristically, do those moralists who oberve and exhibit human conduct and habits—"moralists with discriminating ears, noses, and eyes"—differ entirely from those inventive and imaginative moralists who more questionably engage in interpretation. The passage is significant, for the analogy points to the shift in interest which Nietzsche's whole enterprise represents. The early Nietzsche of *Die Geburt der Tragödie* was sufficiently under Schopenhauer's spell so as to be a cosmologist; for him the tragic perception of Dionysus was a perception of *the real*. But the metaphysical interest induced by the second book of *Die Welt als Wille und Vorstellung* was but a phase, and was at once replaced by the durable concern with the field of human values—with art, with religion, and above all with ethics.

In his earliest phase Nietzsche was influenced equally by Wagner and by Schopenhauer's doctrine of the uses of art in promoting a denial of the will, and the crux of his belief at this point (as he expressed it in the "Preface to Richard Wagner" of *Die Geburt der Tragödie*) is therefore that "art is the highest human task, the true metaphysical activity of this life." And it is under the spell of this conviction that he seeks to found a philosophy of culture in which the Greeks themselves are taken as guarantors of the doctrine that only as "an aesthetic phenomenon" is existence and the world eternally justified. But the ethical interest soon supplants the aesthetic as the bulwark of the Nietzschean humanism, and this is largely due, I think, to the emerging presence of the atheistic premise in Nietzsche's thought.

It is in the parable of the madman in *Die fröhliche Wissenschaft* that the famous dictum "God is dead!" appears: "God is dead! God remains dead! And it is we who have killed him! How shall we console ourselves—the most murderous of all murderers?" But no sooner is the question asked than it is answered. "With what water could we cleanse ourselves? What rites of atonement, what sacred games shall we have to devise? Is not the magnitude of this deed too great for us? *Shall we not ourselves have to become Gods, merely to seem to be worthy of it*?"[25] The inference is obvious, and it is the strategy of every dying supernaturalism. For the atheistic premise generally implies a humanism of sorts—a shift in the locus of the guarantee of values from the divine to the human. It is this shift which the philosophy of Nietzsche has definitively accomplished for the modern world, and it is in this sense if in no other that it is the precursor of Sartre and of every existentialism which emphasizes the "anguish," the "abandonment," and the "despair" of this inevitable displacement.

What is equally significant (if perhaps on the surface less obvious), I think, is the change in the concept of nature which accompanies it. A supernaturalist, or at least a theological, theory of the world often carries with it a vitalistic or at least a matrix view of nature as man's natural home. Partly this is a consequence of reading into existence the governing power of a natural law which is itself the mere reflection of divine fiat. But even more to the point is the metaphysical assumption of a "creationist" perspective. In Plato's *Timaeus* no less than in the *De Caelo* of Aristotle there is an act of making—of imposing form upon matter or of initiating cosmic movement (even if not of creating *ex nihilo* in the Judeo-Christian sense) whereas in Kant or Hume the world is simply *what is there* for sensation and for mental ordering. Two phrases of Spinoza, although they spring from a pantheism which is not quite to our point, yet are relevant in this connection. The world in the making—*natura naturans*—the world as living and created, is God's perspective. The world as there complete—*natura naturata*—the world as dead, as an object, *as merely perceived,* is man's perspective. Thus the passage from a theological to a humanistic point of view entails also the assumption that nature is less a "presence" than an "object." It is this, I think, that Nietzsche seeks to represent when he speaks of nature's "silence."

Except for the passage I have quoted from *Die fröhliche Wissenschaft* and the pervasive natural imagery of *Also sprach Zarathustra* (the purity of mountain air, the solitude of caves, the noonday sun, shimmering mountain streams, the fig tree) there is almost nothing in Nietzsche concerning nature. His themes are rather those of man and of his aesthetic and moral culture: of religion as a corpse, the future of the overman, the origin of moral principles, the nature of human virtues, friendship and rancor, nationalism and race feeling, justice and the beautiful. There is therefore here too a foretaste of the abandonment of nature as a major category of philosophic thought which characterizes the modern world.

The concept of nature as an object, as *natura naturata,* as "merely perceived" which is implicit in the philosophy of Nietzsche, becomes completely explicit in the natural philosophy of Ernst Mach. Mach is the crucial bridge between Hume and Carnap—the philosopher of science whose phenomenalism builds upon Hume's *Treatise* that it may make possible Carnap's *Der logische Aufbau der Welt*. In *The Science of Mechanics* Mach traced the development of a physical science which, once having been grounded in observation, begins the newer deductive phase of its history where theorems are deduced from principles and where formal development alone produces a system of compendant propositions in which "facts" are imbedded so as to be available with "the least intellectual effort." It is clear that Mach is talking about the role of the concept of "uniformity" in the science of mechanics, and that he has in mind the transforming role of that branch of mathematics originating at the close of the seventeenth and the beginning of the eighteenth century dealing with what he called "isoperimetrical problems." But in tracing the contributions of Fermat and Bernoulli, Euler and Lagrange, he is led to meditations upon "theological, animistic, and mystical points of view in mechanics."[26]

After a critique of an earlier "theologizing bent of physics" (best illustrated by Maupertius' "principle of least action") in which the prevailing inclination of inquirers was to find in all physical laws "some particular disposition of the Creator," Mach comments upon the remarkable change which takes place towards the close of the eighteenth century. Now the theological conception gives way to more rationalistic modes of explanation, and the phenomena of nature are taken not as evidences of purposiveness, but as simple givens of experience. It is, of course, natural that physical science should show traces of fetishism in its "pressures" and it "forces," for the fundamental character of thought is impressed by our instinctual feeling of oneness and sameness with nature. But the instinct can be silenced, and in this silencing lies the transformation of modern science. Today careful physical research must lead neither to religious animism nor to a mechanical mythology, but to *an analysis of our sensations*.[27]

It was precisely to this enterprise that Mach himself turned three years later—in his *Die Analyse der Empfindungen* of 1886 —where in his preliminary *Antimetaphysiche Vorbemerkungen* he borrows the resources of Hume to construct a strictly phenomenalist concept of the natural world. Colors, sounds, temperatures, pressures, spaces, times, and the like are mutually connected in manifold ways, and the complexes so conjoined are called bodies. Absolutely permanent, however, they certainly are not. It is the "properties" which count. Thus as different complexes are found to contain common sensory elements, the visible, the audible, the tangible are separated from bodies in reflection to become the givens of experience, and the scientist studies not the gross bodies, but the functional relationships between the sensory elements. "Substance" disappears and only "sensory atoms" remain. However the frequency of analogous occurrences causes us to regard the properties of bodies as "effects" proceeding from permanent nuclei, the world in fact consists only of our sensations. They are the only components of knowledge, and the assumption of permanent nuclei and reciprocal actions between them turns out to be idle and superfluous, if not indeed dangerous to the scientific enterprise.[28]

The deliverances of common sense need then to be revised. Bodies do not produce sensations, but complexes of sensations make up bodies, and if the physicist takes the bodies to be real abiding existences, it is merely because he forgets that they are but thought-symbols *(Gedankensymbole)* for complexes of sensations. The assumption that bodies and our experience are the "effects" of an external world saddles us with a tangle of metaphysical difficulties which it is impossible to unravel. But the specter vanishes at once when we see clearly that all that is valuable to science is *the discovery of functional relationships*[29] and that what we need to know is the network of related experiences.

Mach's phenomenalism is, as we already know, prophetic. And it, too, like the efforts of Reichenbach and Carnap (which it makes possible) in producing a philosophy of science, has practically destroyed the concept of nature. The sensationalist reduction may play into the hands of a mathematical functionalism, but it destroys that very conception of nature *in solido* which Whitehead identifies as the fundamental theme of Wordsworth. Lyric poetry may indeed imply a subjectivity of feeling, but it has never produced a subjectivity like Mach's—where objects dissolve and the whole focus of attention becomes the sensory complex. Wordsworth's "Tintern Abbey" presupposes the substantial furnishing of our natural world: the setting sun, the round ocean, the blue sky, and the living air—and not merely "a sensation of red roundness here now spatially displaced toward the horizon," or "a complex of moments of green wetness moving concentrically," or "this light cool pressure experienced in the nerve endings of the face." And were we to make this Machean substitution in the governing substantives of the poem, we should once more be persuaded of Whitehead's point—"How strained and paradoxical is the view of nature which modern science imposes on our thought."

Mention of Whitehead brings us at last to his nineteenth century analog—to F. H. Bradley and to his "metaphysical" account of nature in *Appearance and Reality* which at once shows the direction in which Whitehead is to move and provides a reasonable third way between the positivistic reduction of nature in Mach and its humanistic neglect by Nietzsche. Particularly with respect to the latter there is a paradox here, and it is that Bradley, an invalid who spent almost his entire life sequestered within the walls of Merton College, Oxford, provides a more sympathetic philosophy of nature than Nietzsche, who so obviously loved Sils-Maria and the snowy solitude of the upper Engadine. But it is the philosophy and not the life which provides the lasting residue.

It is obvious that Bradley has felt the impact of nineteenth century physics. "The word Nature," he says,

> has of course more meanings than one. I am going to use it here in the sense of the bare physical world, that region which forms the object of purely physical science, and appears to fall outside of all mind. Abstract from everything psychical, and then the remainder of existence will be Nature. It will be mere body or the extended, so far as that is not psychical, together with the properties immediately connected with or following from this extension. And we sometimes forget that

> this world, in the mental history of each of us, once had no existence. Whatever view we take with regard to the psychological origin of extension, the result will be the same. There was a time when the separation of the outer world, as a thing apart from our feeling, had not even been begun. The physical world, whether it exists independently or not, is, for each of us, an abstraction from the entire reality.[30]

Bradley does two things here. On the one hand for purposes of definition he accepts the Cartesian dualism. But on the other he shows how it is unreal—an abstraction from the organic character of experience. There comes a time when we all gain the idea of "mere body"—of a world which is independent of the psychical life of any individual, but if this is the Nature of the physicist, it is not the Nature of the common man, and it becomes legitimate to call upon metaphysics to adjudicate their disparate claims.

This Bradley does by showing his preference for wholeness and organicity. The material world is an incorrect, a one-sided, a self-contradictory appearance of the real, and the circular connection between the organism and Nature is not something to be set aside, but to be reinstated. Mere Nature is not real; it is an abstraction which we have separated from "the feeling whole" and enlarged by theoretical necessity and contrivance. For in the end there can be no such thing as a Nature standing apart from some essential relation to finite organisms, not only in its relatedness but in its essence. Each fragment of visible Nature, says Bradley, might, so far as is known, serve as part of some organism not like our bodies. No physical fact which is not *for* some finite sentient being is possible, and this leads easily to a view of Nature which is itself a composite of what Bradley calls (in a phrase which he might have learned from Wordsworth) "finite centers of feeling."

> A Nature without sentience is, in short, a mere construction for science, and it possesses a very partial reality. Nor are the imperceptibles of physics in any better case. Apart from the plain contradictions which prove them to be barely phenomenal, their nature clearly exists but in relation to thought. For, not being perceived by any finite, they are not, as such,

perceived at all; and what reality they possess is not sensible, but merely abstract.[31]

Outside of finite experience there is neither a natural world nor in fact any other world at all, and this leads in its own fashion to the denial of the dualism which Descartes and Locke have contributed to the philosophic legacy of the seventeenth century. Nature is in large part just as it is perceived. Secondary qualities are an actual part of the physical world. The existing thing sugar is actually sweet and pleasant, as well as solid and crystalline, and the beauty of Nature is as much a fact as the hardest of primary qualities. "Everything physical," says Bradley, "which is seen or felt, or in any way experienced or enjoyed, is, on our view, an existing part of the region of Nature; and it is in Nature as we experience it."[32]

But if Bradley is right, if qualities of sense and value are intrinsic to Nature, and if apart from finite minds, the physical world in the proper sense simply does not exist, what then, we must ask, has become of natural science? Bradley's answer is that it remains as before but that its claim to speak for Nature must recede into a more modest pretention. For the object of natural science is neither the ascertainment of ultimate truth, nor are the ideas with which it works intended to set out the true character of reality. The proper question about the principles of science is not whether they possess absolute truth, but whether they are useful and legitimate for an understanding of the sequence and coexistence of phenomena. In the pursuit of this more restricted aim, it is clear that they are both, and the consequence of this reallocation is that we have freed the concept of nature from the narrow restrictions of a positivistic philosophy. Bradley's account of nature means the reestablishment of metaphysics—means, in fact, implicit criticism both of Machean narrowness and Nietzschean neglect. For now we have an enabling act permitting a sober reconsideration of the Wordsworthian premise—of that matrix version of nature which is to find its special genius in the organic metaphysics of Whitehead.

The Secret World of Jean Barois
Notes on the portrait of an age

by Eugen Weber

No work of fiction provides a more faithful, a more deliberately faithful, reflection of the period it describes than Roger Martin du Gard's life of Jean Barois. Written between 1910 and 1913, this is the story of a life drawing to a close in the pre-war years, the Pilgrim's Progress of a positive and idealistic generation, but a Pilgrim's Progress à la mode, in that the tale it tells leads not to triumph but to failure.

Child of the 1860's, Jean Barois breaks loose from the provincial pietism in which he grew up, loses his faith under the spell of scientific studies "where all the universal laws are analyzed without one reference to the name of God," and after an unsatisfactory modernistic stage becomes a militant transformist and agnostic. With a group of like-minded friends, he founds *Le Semeur*, destined to sing "a hymn to progress" and to assert a new élan "against a tired, enervated world." The slogan of the new monthly comes from Lammenais: "Something we do not know is stirring in the world." It is 1896. Within a few months, the Dreyfus controversy breaks out in public and *Le Semeur* takes the van of the Dreyfus campaign, sharing the elation of the struggle and, eventually, the bitterness of victory.

A few years pass. Barois, now in his forties, has become a

leading intellectual of the Left, preaching a scientific relativism. Although he denies "the outdated materialism of the sixties," his irreligion is as firm as ever, his faith in the capacity of thought, pressing forward into the unknown, just as fervent. An odd experience does not shake his faith, but warns him that, however firm the spirit, it might succumb to physical decay and that he must defend the integrity of his thought, be it against his own weakness.

One day, when his cabhorse bolts, he finds himself automatically reenacting Pascal's experience and praying for a miracle to save him from harm. As soon as he can, he draws up a testament embodying those beliefs he wants to assert beyond all possible abdications. He denies free will and the immortal soul. He believes in universal determinism, in evolution, in the capacity of science eventually to explain all phenomena which still remain obscure, in man's need to content himself with limited knowledge and to ignore inaccessible ultimates. He does not want his long struggle on behalf of man's consciousness and his capacity to act, to founder in some recantation born of decrepitude.

But this profession of faith, or perhaps the experience which caused it, marks the beginning of the end. The comradeship and hopes of Dreyfus days have run to seed, the team of *Le Semeur* disintegrates, its subscribers fall away, Barois himself feels discouraged and weary. One of his friends voices the general sentiment of disillusioned *Dreyfusards:* "We had burst the abscess; we counted on recovery, and now gangrene has set in."

The new generation is nothing like the youth of the eighties and the nineties. Not only does it denounce as revolutionary and anarchic the masters of that earlier time, "from Goethe [and Taine] to Renan, Flaubert, Tolstoi, Ibsen, all! . . . ," reject the nineteenth century *in toto*, from 1789 to Jean Jaurès, and reassert "the practical efficacy of faith" in a pragmatic Catholicism. But its language is larded with new and unfamiliar terms, like *discipline, heroism, action, nationalism,* ignored and neglected in his time.

And while the young people he meets shake Barois' faith in the lasting quality of his work, his own daughter, impervious to reason in a shell of simple and simple-minded faith, becomes a nun. Ill health dogs this man who, in his fifties, should have been in his prime. "I have enough," he tells an old friend, "of struggling against a life whose sense escapes me. . . . I cannot resign myself to this emptiness." Abandoning direction of *Le Semeur,* where he had become an anachronism, he returns to his old provincial home, to the pious goose he had married and left long before and, eventually, to the reassurance of the church of his birth. Nothing of the old Barois subsists in this abdication of the mind and will which he had once foreseen; and, when he dies, his widow burns the testament drawn up to speak for the true man. A generation ends, not with a bang and scarcely with a whimper, and Barois embodies its fate.

And yet, a doubt suggests itself. However true a picture this may be, Barois remains—not exactly flat, but one-sided, obsessed by religious problems, fascinated by political ones. Not only does his progress have a monomaniac quality, ignoring many other contemporary concerns, but his public figure (formal even in its more private aspects) reflects few of the interests or the influences he must have felt as student, critic, thinker and, quite simply, as a man of his time. To the cultural historian, Barois is something of a disappointment. Preoccupied by his studies, his marital problems, his editorial duties, his struggle for Dreyfus, and then his health (not to mention his daughter), he finds no time to tell us about the books he reads, the atmosphere in which he moves, the conversations he joins outside his little clique.

After our first elation over this splendid document, our spirits fall. All by itself, it would still be psychologically interesting, but historically meaningless. Indeed, it is only against the historical background that the book acquires its full meaning; and then the story appears true enough, but far too partial, both as concerns its time and as concerns itself. Much of the world where Barois lived is not even hinted at; much of his life is passed under silence.

To put the man's adventure in perspective, to know more of the problems that he faced, a sort of concordance is needed which will show the living world where Barois' passion was played out. In doing this, we shall sketch out the intellectual adventure of his generation.

What was his generation? Barois was born in 1863 or in 1866: we can take our choice. If we go by the evidence of the first few pages, he was twelve years old in 1878; if we prefer a later indication, he was thirty-two in 1895. It does not really matter very much, for either way he becomes the contemporary of figures like Maurice Barrès, born in 1862, Romain Rolland, born in 1866, and Charles Maurras, born in 1868. All grew up about the same time, all came to Paris just when he did, in the eighties. It was a time of tottering faith, with both religious and scientific ultimates exposed to question, disgust with current platitudes—both pious and positivistic—spurring the young to deny all values except that of the Self.

When Barois came to Paris from Buis-la-Dame (Oise) he must have felt much like Romain Rolland, transplanted in October, 1880, from Clamecy, in the Nièvre: "Le peu de foi de province, écroulée. Les gamins de ce temps crachaient dessus. Même nos professeurs (certains, et non des moindres) faisaient rire à ses dépens. Un positivisme materialiste, plat et gras, étalait son huile rance sur l'étang aux poissons."[1]

For Barois, living with his doctor father, giving the best of his time to his medical and pre-medical studies, the new materialism came as a revelation, the dominant determinism appeared sufficient to take the place of God. To contemporaries like Rolland this did not seem enough. Perhaps it was a matter of temperament, perhaps the difference between the humanist and musician of the Ecole Normale and the scientist. What struck Rolland was the disenchantment of ruling materialism. Bourget's *Essais de psychologie contemporaine* (1883-85), which appeared when he was finishing his *lycée,* noted in the French elite "a mortal weariness of life, a drab perception of the vanity of any effort"; and Barrès' *Tâches d'encre* (1884) found in Verlaine "the last stage of debilitation in a worn-out race." From Paris, Vincent Van Gogh apprised his younger sister: "The maladies that afflict us most . . . are melancholy and pessimism." "France is dying," Renan advised a young admirer: "Do not trouble its agony."

With Renan, scepticism reigned over France. And, though he died in 1892—the same year as did Taine, his influence survived. Renan's legacy to the young was, Bodley tells us, the precept to amuse themselves and not to let their pleasures be troubled with vain seekings after truth. J. E. C. Bodley, who knew more about France than any Englishman has ever known, marked this influence and the trend of the times in his long essay on *The Decay of Idealism in France*. So did the French Institute, when it elected William James a corresponding member in 1898. Léon Daudet, another contemporary of Barois, born in 1867, assures us that for the last quarter of the nineteenth century Renan was the god of the Third Republic, and "Renanolatry" more intense even than "Hugolatry": "He had even become popular . . . admired without being read."[2] Though people did read *The Future of Science,* written in 1848 but not published until 1889, they might prefer Barrès's skit of the same year, *Eight Days with M. Renan,* in which ironic discrimination, the scepticism of hungry youth picked at the great sceptic himself.

Others contributed to the vogue of scepticism. Flaubert had died in 1880, but his spirit survived in his nephew, Maupassant, and the *grossièretés* of contemporary naturalism (*L'Ilustration,* March 20, 1886 *dixit);* in the *Temptation of St. Anthony,* required reading for poetic youths like Barrès and Stanislas de Guaita; but above all in *Buvard and Pécuchet*. The literary young, Eugène-Melchior de Vogüé assured a friend, knew this breviary by heart.[3] Under Flaubert's aegis they could indulge their own well-developed scorn of contemporary nonsense.

It was, as Barrès would recall, as indeed he never ceased to recall, "a generation disgusted with many things, perhaps with everything, except playing with ideas...." Of these they had only too many—and too much. In 1889, Jules Renard (1864-1910) felt that it was time for a book, *Le Nihilisme,* to sum up the experience of his kind. And in the first of his book-length manifestos, Barrès drew one conclusion of their plight: "Pending the time when our masters have reconstructed some certainties for us, it would be proper to stick to the only reality, to the Self."[4]

Barois, if no one else, should be enough to tell us that other realities and other certitudes existed all the same, and chief of these was science. Léon Daudet remembers that when pursuing his own medical studies, betwen 1885 and 1892, the foremost scientific dogma was that of evolution, *"tarte à la crème de la biologie, de la psychologie, de la philosophie, de la médecine."* Its corollary was the belief in "progress and science, ever beneficent, pacific, and devoted to human felicity." This idea of evolution as a development of matter into ever more complex wholes and even into "mind" would become a sort of truism by the 1890's when Barois had to give up teaching natural science at Venceslas (i. e. Stanislas) College in Paris. The young science teacher, admired by his students, had shocked his Catholic superiors by insisting on the essential importance of transformism, "whose law, dominating all, dominates also the evolution of human consciousness."

Another law was that recognised by the disciples of Marx or, more immediately, of Jules Guesde. The older French socialism —of Considérant, Louis Blanc, Proudhon—had been largely wiped out after the Commune; and, while this meant that workers lay quiescent through the seventies, it also meant that the way was free for Marxism. By 1879, a workers' congress had adopted it as official doctrine. One can agree with René Rémond that French socialism originated as a defensive reaction against the violent changes inflicted by industrialization. From this point of view, socialism (like the anarchism so active in the late nineteenth century) was less a vision of the future than "the disguised expression of a nostalgic attachment to the past."[5] Moreover, the overwhelming fact is that by the 1880's the workers' movement scarcely rises out of the ruins of the Commune. Freedom of reunion was only granted in 1881, of syndical organization in 1884. The rise of labor begins in 1893, when fifty Socialists were returned to the Chamber, or in 1895, when the General Confederation of Labor (C.G.T.) appeared to assert syndicalist liberties; but its political power was slight before 1900.

Intellectually, of course, the question seems different. To those who were hungry for certainty, eager for justice, Marxism offered positive analyses and laws. But the socialism that caught on was less Marxist than humanist, romantic, a new-fangled extension of the cult of the Self. "Here we are," wrote Barrès in 1890, "on the hospitable shores of socialism. It is a nice place to tarry, albeit from necessity. It is our Jersey." Jersey, of course, was the temporary exile not only of Victor Hugo, but also of Boulanger. But Jersey, for Barrès, was something else as well. The hero of his *Un Homme libre* had found there "the last word of true sincerity, the formula ennobled by the high culture of the Self: For oneself! . . ."

For these young men, socialism—which Barrès explored at length in *L'Ennemi des lois* (1892)—was less an enterprise of social reform than one more aspect of self-cultivation. Politics provided *"de quoi nourrir mon imagination, ma sensibilité, mon âme."*[6] And it was something else: a stick to beat the bourgeois, the capitalist, the gross materialist under whose barbarian eyes the Self was bound to wither. Therein lies the secret of early national socialism in *La Cocarde* (1894), and even the socialism of so many bourgeois intellectuals. Defense of Self, aggression against barbarians, taking sides against the brutes one knew and for those one did not know so well—not well at all, in fact; but always bearing in mind that Marxism, like materialism, is no ultimate answer. Thus, the bibliography of Marc-Elie Luce, who would play such an important part in the life of Barois and the fortunes of *Le Semeur,* shows that, after a compendious study of religious faith, he had published in succession: *Les régions supérieures du socialisme, Le Sens de la vie,* and *Le Sens de la mort.* The wealthy, after all—as André Malterre points out—are in the best position to know that when material needs are satisfied their sensitivity still calls for other satisfactions; that even *mal au coeur* cannot remove the *vague à l'âme.*

The fancy stylist who dedicated his *Un Homme libre* to *"quelques collégiens de Paris et de province,"* proposed a rich boy's philosophy: to seek without hope of finding, to take pleasure in experiments not in results, to amuse oneself with means careless of the end—these are not recipes for proletarian action or satisfaction, let alone class war. The war that Barrès fought was therefore scarcely in the socialist tradition, and its means were typified by his nihilist hero's answer when asked what he meant to do: *"On pourrait faire une publication . . ."*[7]

This, apparently, was also the feeling of Jean Barois. When ready for action, one brings out a review. To do this one needs, as an aged mentor mentions in *Sous l'oeil des barbares,* "*quelques rentes et de la santé.*" And Barois' world, like that of Barrès, is a world of rentiers, where the small capital necessary to start and the small losses involved in running a review could be found and covered by one or two or three *fils de famille* just out of college, in a position to indulge a literary or polemical whim as easily as they could rent a *garçonnière* to satisfy some other. But if little reviews multiplied, the reason was more than just the low cost of their printing and the ease with which the cost could be raised. For most of the century stringent press laws had limited publications. Restraints had been eased in the last years of the Second Empire, but the Republic, mindful of the Commune, returned to greater stringency. It was only when freedom of the press triumphed, in 1881, that small reviews began to proliferate on the conjunction of a prosperous and disputatious middle class and a tolerant political regime.

But if André Malterre was nothing but an egotistic dilettante, surely Barois might be expected to do better. Yet his *Semeur* (1895) seems concerned above all else with moral and ideological questions, entirely ignoring Marx, the C.G.T., or any concrete aspect of the workers' movement. Its chief campaigns before Dreyfus are anticlerical, and after him the same. At least Barrès, when he founded *La Cocarde* concomitant with *Le Semeur,* took notice of current politics, greeting the resignation of President Casimir-Périer as "one of the moments of the Social Revolution," and calling for the organization of labor (which would come that year with the C.G.T., an institution most men of letters seem to have ignored).

I speak, you see, only of possibilities and activities within Barois' ken, leaving aside, for instance, Catholics or simple reactionaries whom he could glimpse from afar as dark and hostile forces. But, while a revolutionary change was preparing in that quarter too, the change in public mood of which Barois must have been aware had been precipitous in the late eighties. Tired of flat realism, jaded with sordid naturalism, empty of faith, uneasy in its self-conscious dilettantism, the educated youth of the mid-eighties sought for sensations, for some warming passion or *petite secousse,* far from the *"recherche prétentieuse, byzantine, et glaciale"* a critic had denounced in the *Décadents.* "Lacking faith," wrote Vogué in 1886, this youth "has in the highest degree a sense of mystery, and there lies its distinctive trait."[8]

The same year, 1886, saw the publication of Moréas' Symbolist Manifesto, expression of a movement which Stéphane Mallarmé had "endowed with a sense of mystery," and which took its inspiration from Baudelaire's invitation to strange journeys into the unknown:

Plonger au fond du gouffre, Enfer ou Ciel, qu'importe?
Au fond de l'Inconnu pour trouver du nouveau.

The poet, Rimbaud had said, must be a *seer:* Bergson was soon to certify this from, perhaps, a more authoritative quarter. And nothing could be more welcome than the suggestion that beyond the drab and dreary crust of everyday conventions a rich reality lurked, on which initiates could feed the spirit, in which they could steep the Self. This sense of mystery could lead some people to strange pastures. Faced with the deadlock between theological and scientific world views, many took refuge in spiritualistic cults which plumbed the depths that disbelief avoided without quite ignoring. "Glory and praise to Satan in the highest," wrote Baudelaire, and it was near him that many sought their way. Doctors, artists, writers—Barrès, Stanislas de Guaita, Maurras, Daudet, Eric Satie, the Marquis de Morès (and his American wife)— dabbled in occultism, graphology, palmistry, telepathy, and mysticism.[9]

For some, as for Huysmans, satanism would lead to God: one source of aesthetic inspiration to another. Others need only follow the Baudelairean tradition to its Christian and catastrophic end, like Léon Bloy: "I await the cossacks and the Holy Ghost." The Catholic revival of the nineties remains outside my scope, as it was beyond that of Barois. But, clearly, Leo XIII's encyclical, *Rerum Novarum* (1891) and his call to Catholics to rally the Republic (1892), coming at this time of spiritual disarray, suggested the latent possibilities of a Church no longer sourly turned against the world.

But if one avenue deserves particular attention as the chief competitor of the Church and its major foe, it is Freemasonry. Freemasonry provided a spiritualistic (sometimes even satanistic) anti-Church, opposing a doctrine of its own, "a religion of Good and . . . of the spirit," to the harsh intolerances of traditional creeds. There were symbolist Masons, like Oswald Wirth (secretary of Stanislas de Guaita, the occultist), and Marius Lepage (director of a review, *Le Symbolisme).* There would be deeply occultist Masons, like René Guénon (1886-1951), who sought to renew the doctrine by an appeal to oriental tradition. And one of the directions in which Jules Romains' *Men of Good Will* look for a faith—(Vol. VII: *Recherche d'une Eglise)*— would be the *loge,* its solidarity and its ideas.

Characteristically enough, however, just as spiritualism signaled itself chiefly by its frauds, Masonry would make its greatest impact in politics and business; where it appears, invested indeed with a mysterious aura, but chiefly as a mutual aid society serving the material interests of its members. M. Homais had been a Mason. By 1900, says Gordon Wright, almost every Radical deputy was a Mason, too.

This being so, it is not entirely surprising to find the friends of Jean Barois ignoring the possibilities of Masonic influence. But, certainly, many of Barois' readers must have been members of a *loge*.[10] And, at a time when the Masonic conspiracy was being denounced from so many quarters, they could not fail to appreciate the discreet (or indifferent) silence of *Le Semeur*.

There seem to have been other strange gaps however in *Le Semeur's* pages, omissions which a wise discretion does not suffice to explain. Vogüé's judgment on the young generation's sense of mystery, quoted above, was formulated in the Foreword of his *Roman russe:* a book which would acquaint everybody (in Péguy's sense of eight or nine hundred people) with these "enormous" men, the great Russian novelists, deeply realistic and just as deeply aware of invisible and unknown forces, who could suggest a reconciliation between realism and idealism. It was Barois' contemporary, Rolland, who carried the Russian novel into the Ecole Normale which he entered in 1886, who insisted that the library buy Tolstoi, Dostoievski, and Goncharov, and who even set out to translate a Tolstoi short story from German into French.[11] It would be another contemporary, Barrès, who, a few years later, raised up the classic French tradition to oppose the romantic admirers of the Russians.

Barois, however, remained outside the debate, vouchsafing not a glance in its direction. The critical columns of his *Semeur* would be devoted to works of "positive philosophy and *practical* sociology." Outside of that, art for art's sake still reigned, even against Tolstoi, through the good offices of Cresteil, one of the founding members, who was well enough informed to know Tolstoi's essay, *What is Art?*, two years before its publication of 1897. Cresteil, however, leaned more to William Morris than to the Russian's moralistic nihilism. His social concern is aesthetic, but the aestheticism is tinged with social awareness. Insisting on the artist's duty to think only of beauty (for only the disinterested emotion is truly creative), he affirmed, nevertheless, that the useful inevitably results from such an aesthetic approach. For Cresteil had turned Morris upside down: the artist need not concern himself with the social results of his work, but the results of honest, dedicated work are bound to be socially significant.

Cresteil was fated to commit suicide in 1913, when he realized the vanity of his ideas. Marcel Proust, who in his time had shared them, contented himself with translating Ruskin, before going on to write a novel.

It was, I think, because they surveyed the world from this elevated if somewhat dated promontory, that the mind of Jean Barois and the pages of his review show little trace of Tolstoi and none of Nietzsche. And if, by 1896, the Russians might not seem novel enough to interest a monthly, Nietzsche at least would seem to deserve their attention, since translations of his works, and articles concerning him, were growing in number after 1892. The very year *Le Semeur* was founded, Hugues Rebell had presented the German prophet as counterbalancing a certain *"évangélisme Tolstoïsant,"* and had insisted that "no more dangerous opponent existed of the sordid socialism which threatens to ruin everything we love . . . ."[12] Such an ambiguous figure would surely attract the attention of intellectuals on the qui vive,[13] and yet our friends seem to have missed him. One might conclude that the group of *Le Semeur* lacked the most elementary intellectual curiosity.

The causes of their silence may be found in the brief intervention by Harbaroux, the historian and librarian of the Arsenal, who, at the founding meeting, insisted that any sociology entertained by the new review should be of a *practical* kind. The term is a clue which should lead us to the master of practical sociology, Emile Durkheim, himself only a few years older than Barois. Like Durkheim, these ebullient but earnest young men found little time to spare from the task of building a kind of secular morality which would help reestablish order and stability on a convincing basis. While Barrès and Rolland had dallied among the poets, men like Barois had been absorbed by scientific studies, men like Harbaroux by their medieval charters. Their positive discipline made them look down on lighter fare. Whatever their later views, in the eighties they must have resembled Durkheim, in whose writings of those years "a definite anti-intellectualistic strain recurs frequently and unmistakably."[14] Like Barrès, Durkheim rejected systems. But where Barrès concluded that "the only truths that touch us are those that make us cry," Durkheim thought that the truths that matter are those that make us good. Where, for the dynamic of a better life, Barrès looked to individuals, he looked to society, "focus of moral life," whose "true function is to create the ideal."

The major problem thus became not the analysis of sensations but of society, and the social question itself, as we have seen with *Le Semeur,* was focused on the need for "positive moral direction." *Le Semeur* would have agreed with Durkheim that "the social question . . . is not a question of money or of force; it is a question of moral agents. What dominates is not the state of our economy, but the state of our morality." And Henri Peyre's description of what Durkheim wanted would apply equally to Barois and to his friends: "To derive an ethic from the science of society, to evolve rules of conduct, characterized by obligation and desirability, founded on science."[15]

This had also been the dream of Renan, who hid it behind his smiling scepticism. It had been the dream of Taine, whose cultural sociology had been useful in its time. But Taine, like Adrien Sixte, had gone too far. He had insisted that science could be applied not only to culture but to the soul itself, and this opened the door to dangerous excesses. In 1889 Paul Bourget denounced not only the delicate soundings of the soul Barrès advocated, but also the steelier probes of science. Moreover, despite his friendship for the younger man, Bourget saw that, at least in their common circle, the refined intellectual epicurean was more to be feared than the scientific positivist: "Ce nihiliste délicat, comme il est effrayant à rencontrer et comme il abonde! A vingt-cinq ans il a fait le tour de toutes les idées . . . ."[16]

But if Bourget's *Disciple,* and even more the long preface with which it opened, was so significant, if Bourget's insistence on responsibility and his denial of materialistic determinism had the "unique and decisive influence" they did, it was because, as Victor Giraud would explain, they marked the "precise moment when the generation to which Bourget belongs detaches itself from the preceding generation." This, strangely enough, is just what Vogüé had claimed for his *Roman russe,* three years before.[17]

If one wants to be precise, it was less the generation born in the fifties (like Bourget and Vogüé) that welcomed the ideas such works suggest, than the generation of the sixties and the seventies. The sad tale of Robert Greslou and Adrien Sixte did so well because the doors opened of their own accord. There was no need to batter. At the *Semeur,* at the Normale, even at the Sorbonne, responsibility, commitment, and, increasingly, those mysterious forces positive science ignored, were making their way. In 1888, still in his cloister of the rue d'Ulm, Rolland had noted: "I see a time coming when the word *intuition* will have a singularly broader, more scientific, and more precise sense than it has today."[18] The year 1889 is not only the date of *Le Disciple,* but of the *Essai sur les données immédiates de la conscience.*

It has not been sufficiently remarked how closely Bergson's "intuition" resembles certain Barrèsian techniques. It appears as a highly refined application of mind, a unique kind of emotion or sense by which, if we press deeply enough into our own selves, a new, integral reality may be revealed. It might be said that pure thought, when sufficiently acute, becomes "intuition"—beyond good and evil—and perhaps this is the essence of the contemporary search, not only in the great trinity of Nietzsche, Bergson, and Freud, but also among the artists and writers who, sharing the same disillusion with existing symbols, sought by much simpler means (pure thought being outside their province but "experience" very close) to express similar conclusions. Symbolism, impressionism, expressionism are all cases in point.

Like that of Barrès, Bergson's *oeuvre* is also highly critical: "My books," he would admit, "have always been the expression of a dissatisfaction, of a protest."[19] Both men despaired of language and of the use of words, and both shared certain intuitions which prefigure Freud . . . and André Breton.

Marcel Raymond has quoted Bergson's remarks on the artist's task, which is "to reveal nature" by "capturing something which has no longer anything in common with the spoken word, certain rhythms of life . . ." that Bergson calls "a music." Raymond comments that Bergson's whole sense of life is musical and his philosophy akin to the poetry of the symbolists whose first purpose, on the evidence of Mallarmé and Valéry, was to recapture the musical and *evocative* quality of poetry. This may be nothing new, but here is the interesting thing: from Bergson's point of view, one use of this evocative music would be to *"endormir les puissances actives ou plutôt résistantes de notre personnalité,"* so that we can get past this surface layer to a reality truer and more profound. Of course, this brings to mind the experiments of André Breton and Philippe Soupault. But it may be compared with a similar recipe coming from Barrès, who speaks of Venice, which he loved above all else in life: "The fever I would catch there was very dear to me, for it increased clairvoyance to the point where my deepest unconscious life and my psychic life mingled to serve as an immense reservoir of power. And I followed my most indistinct and obscure feelings with such acuteness that I often discerned in them the future in the process of taking shape."[20]

The coincidence is striking, and yet appropriate if we remember contemporary concerns. St. Paul said that the visible is the manifestation of the invisible. So did Baudelaire. This perception would be the essence of Bergson's thought, and of most modern art as well: "All this is in us, all this is around us, and yet we perceive none of it distinctly. Between nature and ourselves—

indeed, between us and our own consciousness, a veil intervenes, thick for the mass of men, light, almost transparent, for the artist and the poet." The veil is one of habit, conventions, and ready-made concepts, such as Bouvard, helped by Pécuchet, had set out to collate. This is where intuition comes in, which Bergson opposes to analysis. Analysis proceeds by addition, by combining partial, fragmentary views. Intuition grasps things "in a single simple view." The one deals with signs and labels, the other seeks "an integral experience." The artist's intuition—his passionate vision of things—is of the latter kind. He does not analyze or describe or explain—he reveals: "The highest ambition of art is to reveal nature to us."[21] *"Liegt nicht der Kern der Natur Menschen im Herzen?"*

But there were serious dangers in such views. Bergson had adopted the term "intuition" reluctantly, because "intelligence" seemed to suggest not "understanding," but a purely logical linear approach he wanted to avoid. When his *Essai* appeared, hidebound mechanism was in the saddle, though its determinism no longer provided the security of yore. Many have testified to the *"efficacité libératrice"* of Bergson's work. Yet it could be taken also in what became the most popular interpretation: as a cult of activism, and of intuitions sprung from our true nonintellectual self. And this was one more ground on which Bergson and Barrès would, willy-nilly, meet. It was no coincidence that Eugen Diederichs, proto-Nazi and crackpot, was the German publisher of Bergson, in whom he saw a mysticism, a "new irrationalistic philosophy," for a world that could only progress in opposition to rationalism.[22]

Of course, none of this took effect at once. Robert Junod, whom Bergson burnt like fire, nevertheless read Taine as well. When Duhamel started his medicine in 1902, his masters in biology still "preached transformism . . . an evangel, not a curriculum."[23] At the Sorbonne, Durkheim, Lévy-Bruhl, Frédéric Rauh opposed Bergson in the name of positive science. As late as 1906 Lévy-Bruhl would assure Bergson of his faith in the solidity and the future of positivism. But by then such views began to seem anachronistic. Even Barois (probably in 1903) found the scientific materialism of an earlier day "petty and incomplete." Like Durkheim, sociology taught him relativism. A younger generation would go further: their relativism became as "positive" as the scientific determinism of yore, their pragmatic affirmations as intolerant as the mechanistic dogma. Pragmatism justified prejudice no less than scientism.

At the end of *Un Homme libre,* Barrès concluded to abandon his ivory tower for active life which alone could satisfy the appetites: "I have decided to build in the midst of my time. . . . Among men I have found toys [to amuse my higher Self], to gain respite from my baser self discontented with inaction." Parallel to art for art's sake a new cult was growing, of action for action's sake, which took longer to decay. It is easy to see how idle and disoriented youth would welcome a rag, something to do, and, moreover, the chance to *find* themselves in the midst of action, the gesture preceding and confirming the vestigial thought; or, better still, stirring the precious cinders of emotion.

Barrès had noted the rapid surge in him of the desire, the haste, to plunge body and soul into some nonsensical enterprise: "Ah! the attraction of the irretrievable, in which I have always sought lasting repose. . . ."[24] It is this availability of a public, bored with the regime, harassed by disintegrating certitudes, like ice floes in the spring, looking for new masters now that the old were being discredited—it was this that helped the rise of Boulanger. 1886-89 was a crucial time in which Vogüé, Barrès, Bergson, and Bourget all publicized the different aspects of a dawning mood. They were not alone. It was in September, 1886, that *Le Figaro* published Moréas' *Symbolist Manifesto,* with its talk of hallucinations, shadowy outlines, subjective deformation; in October, that Rimbaud's *Illuminations* came out, answering Baudelaire, heralding Breton; on Christmas Day, in fine, that Paul Claudel escaped "the materialistic servitude," the "hard concatenation of effects and causes," in a vision of "the innocence, the eternal childhood, of God." But the same year had also marked the miners' first really violent strike and, more important, the explosive rise to popularity of General Boulanger. The Boulangist fever would go on growing until 1889. "On ne résiste pas à ces courants inexplicables," wrote the unsympathetic and respectable *Illustration,* "on les subit."

One of the first to submit, to plunge body and soul into the nonsensical enterprise that he had wished for, was Barrès, nowise affected by apparent contradictions: *"Ne point subir! C'est le salut quand nous sommes pressés par une société anarchique. . . ."*[25]

Clearly, salvation lay not only in self-affirmation, but in submission too, or, rather, in active service. In the *appel au soldat* many disparate tendencies met to satisfy a vague but pressing need for action. The most striking thing about the Boulangist adventure is that it had no aim, no purpose, and in the end no leader—the general was a flag waved by a variety of enthusiasts, a balloon blown up by the hot air of passions not his own. As the adventure went, so did the song. Barrès's appropriately named *Roman de l'énergie nationale* (1897-1902) attacks many things but affirms only one: the virtue of energetic self-assertion. Years later, Barrès looked back nostalgically at himself and his fellow-Boulangists: "Comme nous modelions les âmes! J'avais plaisir à me dire: je suis de cette race des artistes." It is as if the Boulangist crush were a hygienic exercise, a youthful passion in which all men see but the image of their own self-love.

Politically, however, the Boulangist fever was to leave its mark. In politics, as in culture, 1886-89 appears a watershed: not only the prelude to a conservative consolidation (the *Ralliement* dates from 1892) against which radicals of the Left and Right would henceforth campaign, not just the root of persistent hatreds and assaults against a republic sapped by recurrent scandals, but origin of the myth of national decadence and of the cult of energy which alone could cure it. Thus, action, gratuitous in its merely intellectual aspect, became a necessity for the nation, a kind of spiritual gymnastics with which to get the people into shape.

Into shape for what? For action at its most intense: for war. We know that the decade before 1914 was full of war scares, but we forget how anguished, how oppressed by fear the eighties and the nineties must have been. The year 1886 was one of war scares, sabre-rattling on both sides of the Rhine, repeated incidents along the Franco-German border, each magnified by a susceptible and nervous press.

On September 25, 1886, *L'Illustration* notes the launching of a war balloon equipped to carry machine guns and bombs: "A great step forward in the art of turning men into a pulp." In February, 1887, a painter expresses fear of the impending war: *"C'est que je voudrais avoir fini mon tableau. . . ."* In April of that year, Gabriel Monod could assure his students at the Ecole Normale that war would be upon them in the space of two weeks.

"The future will find it hard to conceive the moral oppression under which we have spent our youth, we the generation of 1866-72," notes Romain Rolland in January, 1888: "Death, for us, is ever present and its form precise: it is war. Since 1875, the country lives in the shadow of war. Since 1880 war is certain, imminent. Soldiers sacrificed in advance, we camp wherever we may find ourselves, our suitcases never unpacked, awaiting the order to go at any moment. Impossible to plan for the future! I do not know if I shall ever finish the work I have begun, develop the idea I have conceived. . . ." A decade later there has been no respite: "The tragedy of our time is the uncertainty of the world's future, the approach of catastrophe, and the anguished impossibility of doing anything about it."[26] Which only goes to show that purgatory is always someone's *belle époque*.

When time presses and catastrophe looms nigh, those who do not give in to despair have good reason to deploy all their forces, hasten to pile Pelion [upon] Ossa, to leave at least some trace of their existence behind. Moreover, the "decadence" which had been a literary affectation of the eighties had, by the nineties, become a national concern. Abroad, Nietzsche, Kipling, offered lessons of energy. Travelers returned appalled to have seen

France from a world perspective looking much smaller, much weaker, less imposing, than they had ever imagined. Sailing in 1894 to take up a command in Tonkin, the most clear-sighted of French soldiers, Lyautey, reported back the bitter discovery "of what little importance we have, and how little we are taken seriously." Covering the revived Olympic Games of 1896, a young reporter was equally dismayed: "Sorti de mon pays," wrote Charles Maurras on his return from Athens, "je le vis enfin tel qu'il est. Que je fus effrayé de le voir si petit!"[27]

Falling birthrate, stagnant production, lagging enterprise, parliamentary chaos, political divisions, seemed patent proofs of a decline symbolized by the defeat of 1871, the corruption that launched periodic scandals and continuing intellectual anarchy. John Bowditch argues that in the years after 1890, Bergson's *élan vital,* interpreted largely in terms of French vitality or will to action, is "a rationalization of weakness," due to the growing sense of national inferiority: a compensatory myth. It certainly affected not only military thought and the nationalist revival of the pre-war decade but, as Bowditch shows, the weak and ineffective syndical organization of those years.[28] If this is so, perhaps the insistence on order and discipline which so nonplussed Barois in his decline were similiarly compensatory phenomena. The pressure of an anarchic society could be withstood only by self-assertion, suggested Barrès. But this only made confusion worse confounded, adding one more factor to the existing anarchy. The alternative was to put an end to anarchy by imposing one solution over the others, and that, the one best suited to society as a whole, not intellectual, not subjective except in the largest sense, not universalistic, but pragmatic: based on the profound reality of society and race—*la terre et les morts.*

Already the hero of *Un Homme libre* realized that "une race qui prend conscience d'elle-même s'affirme aussitôt en honorant ses morts." The barbarians alien to the Self became barbarians alien to the race, to the nation. If the free man had best realize himself in society, then the Self could now assert itself only at the expense of aliens. Traditional values would provide the positive basis of national morality.

In a comparison of Lyautey and Barrès, Georges Hardy speaks of the latter's traditionalism as "a life-belt grasped by a man in distress, the refuge of a romantic against metaphysical anguish, the last recourse of a man who has lost religious faith and fears the misery of a total scepticism." He is probably right, and his judgment might well apply to others than Barrès, even in their recourse to Catholicism. It is because Lyautey was *rooted* that he did not need to fall back on artificial appeals to this or that rationalization of an absent faith.[29]

For Barrès, however, as for Jean Barois, the ambient disorder and uncertainty would be too much to bear. Any port was good in the storm, even though the would-be positive assertion only added another note to the contemporary cacophony. After the turmoil of the eighties, after the tumult of the nineties, the men of letters took refuge in revelation. They had roamed too long. The nation, the Church, offered integral explanations, a passionate vision that assuaged doubt.

Symbolism was dying with the century. In the *Nouvelle Revue,* Camille Mauclair had published a long article with a significant title: "Souvenirs du Symbolisme, 1884-1897." In the *Revue des Deux Mondes,* René Doumic greeted 1900 with the "Account of a Generation," and concluded that "the fine days of dilettantism are definitely past."[30] To the weary fighters of *Le Semeur,* Marc-Elie Luce quoted the words of Eugène Carrière: "The violence of men is like the great winds of nature: it swells and grows like them, then dies down and disappears, leaving the seeds to do their work. . . . For us, our task is done; the realization of what we had passionately hoped for is not for us."

So much for Jean Barois—at least for the moment. The question now is why he failed; why, by 1900, the high hopes of the last few years seemed to be lost in failure; why, in the confusion of the century's closing decades, well-meaning intellectuals were so ineffective; and why there was confusion in the first place. It is clear enough that doubt over the possibility of arriving at unique positive truths made for scepticism, eclecticism, subjectivism, and that—paradoxically—the multiple profession of subjective truths would lead to the peremptory assertion of pragmatic actions.

To the persistent observer, however, the multiplicity of endeavors, the irony of their fate, are all less striking than the ambient frustration. Seldom have intellectuals been more articulate, more insistent, more numerous, more diverse. Seldom have they reflected so faithfully the variants and the vagaries of educated opinion. Yet, like proportional suffrage, seldom have they been more ineffectual—perhaps, like proportional suffrage, because their very representativeness made for division, dispersion, and abortion.

The role of the intellectual in the life of the Third Republic has been noticed by most observers; and certainly few societies have know a more active and self-conscious intelligentsia, or paid more attention to it. After 1879, when the doubtful days of the regime were done, when MacMahon had resigned and the Republicans really took over, teachers, writers, journalists, burst into public life. The new regime built its foundations in the schools; and the schools were not only hatcheries of a republican electorate and an increasingly literate public, but nurseries of republican politicians to staff the *République des professeurs*.

After 1881, a series of laws made education secular, compulsory, and free. The provincial normal schools, *"des véritables séminaires,"* turned out legions of *instituteurs* who would affirm the new civic morality—material, limited, and lay—against the nefarious trinity of Church, monarchy, and alcohol with missionary zeal. "Like the priests," said Marcel Pagnol's father, "we labor for the future life: but, for us, it is the life of others."[31] The results of their labor would be felt in the nineties. The pupils they turned out would vote in 1898 and 1902, just when the conservative Right endured its worst defeats, to confirm the judgment of the great educational reformers of the eighties.

But by this time the civics that were taught in school were becoming threadbare. To a new generation, the religion of science was beginning to seem insufficient, the example of their elders seemed to deny the lessons of civic morality, the ultimate subjectivism of neo-Kantian pedagogues left in its wake a trail of *déracinés*, uprooted from the solid certainties of habit, unready for the solitary agony of free decision, swinging between inertia and rebellion without a cause. The affirmations of an earlier age now sounded hypocritical and often were: the tribute paid by indifference to comformity and not the call to a better life.

In attacking Adrien Sixte, Bourget was not arguing against theorists and armchair philosophers but against men of power, whose influence really counted in the world. Barrès made this clear when he made a professor-in-politics the villain of *Les Déracinés*. The influence of teachers made the anti-intellectual reaction more intense than if it had been part of mere theoretical debate. Bourget's appeal of 1889 articulates a real and growing resentment of the "anarchic" effects of modern ideas; and if his later works often present the anti-hero as professor *(L'Etape, Le Tribun)* or as young *ideologue* (*La Barricade*), no one found this out of proportion.

This prominence of *ideologists* and their extraordinary activity in the eighties and nineties may be seen as an explosion of energies set free by the press law of 1881, encouraged by the schools, and spurred by the great debates over science, religion, and society then in full swing. The same issues or others just as stimulating had been up before, but on the eve of 1789 the public had been restricted in numbers, and after 1815 it had been restricted in freedom. After 1881, these drawbacks removed, the exhilaration of freedom made for a wealth of polemics feeding on every issue and inevitably creating new ones as they went along.

Obviously then, the numbers of the public and the freedom of the actors are crucial factors in our story. But possibly the terms might be inversed, and a glance cast at the number of the actors and the freedom of the public. For the confusion that we have noted in those years is largely the result of the *number* of voices, all speaking at once, all saying different things. And their ineffectual efforts may result from some check upon either their reasoning, or their conclusions.

If we try to account for the sheer number of groups and coteries and publications, we find, as I suggested earlier, that the intellectual activity of the time is staffed by the middle classes—mostly young men of independent means who do not have to work, who fill some sinecure (like Marcel Proust who, at twenty-five, is appointed unpaid assistant in the Bibliothèque Mazarine, immediately applies for leave, and is dismissed after five years, four of which had been spent on leave)—or whose duties, in the family firm, a ministerial cabinet, in the courts, leave ample time for other pursuits.[32]

The golden age of the intellectual is also the golden age of the *rentier;* and for this there are good economic reasons. The quarter-century, 1848-73, had seen a great spurt of economic activity and a rise in prices in England, Germany, and France. This period of expansion, exhilarating for some, but hard on people living on fixed incomes, would end in 1873 and be followed by an equally long slump, ending only in the mid-nineties. For France this meant that the beginnings of the Third Republic, far from re-editing the prosperity of the Empire, saw a general slowing down; prices fell, and so did profits. On the other hand, the real income of the salaried and working classes tended to rise, and so did the revenue of those who held bonds and stocks. Industry stagnated. Clapham tells us that the "industrial revolution" began in France about 1895. Wholesale prices had fallen from 124 in 1873 (taking 1913=100) to 71 in 1896. Securities, however, followed a different trend. According to P. Vigreux, their value had doubled (in the case of those with variable revenue) or even tripled (in the case of those with fixed revenues), especially when the variation in prices is considered. As a recent study of the period puts it, the years between 1873 and 1896 would be a blessed period for all those who see their buying power rising rapidly: retired people, savers, creditors of fixed sums, holders of French and foreign state bonds, and so on. Of all those, in fact, who play a passive role in economic life.[33]

And while circumstances encouraged the least active section of economic society, they also discouraged some of the potentially active from turning to affairs from which little profit was to be expected. The most dynamic among the young discovered that advancement lay in non-economic enterprises of a political or cultural nature: in the newspapers, the publishing or entertainment world, the university, parliament, *salons* and *cénacles*. The very situation which suggested this also made it possible, by providing them or their parents with the revenues on which they could subsist, and by creating a public which, even in the absence of wider audience, enabled them to persist by taking in each other's washing.

Meanwhile, the possessing class, the *grande bourgeoisie* which had dominated France for most of the century, found itself disoriented, losing confidence, and opposed only a weak resistance to criticism both theoretical and political. Its economic supremacy had been shaken by the depression, its political power had declined at the close of the seventies with the triumph of republican parliamentarism and of the middle classes over the "notables." The Third Republic, at its beginning, had been conservative. The resignation of MacMahon in 1879 and his succession by Jules Grévy were the concrete symbols of a new regime. In August, 1880, a partial renewal of the General Councils of the French Departments would leave the "notables" of the Right with only twenty-one councils out of eighty-four. In January, 1881, the Republicans took over 20,000 communes out of 36,000. In Périgord, Marshal Canrobert, hero of the Imperial wars (1850-70), was beaten by a veterinarian. "End of an epoch," says René Rémond, "but not of a society...."[34]

Herein lies an important source of contemporary unease and dissatisfaction. The old "society" lived on, but it became increasingly isolated, and quite deliberately so. Judges resigned their posts, officers resigned their commissions, "notables" withdrew to their local spheres, families and factions cut themselves off behind the high walls of their great houses. It was an internal emigration and, strangely enough, this was not limited to great families alone. It is interesting to hear one of Bergson's favorite disciples, Gilbert Maire, describe bourgeois families like his own (his father was librarian at the Sorbonne) which closed their doors to deputies and ministers, *"gens de mauvaise compagnie et de réputation équivoque,"* to whom one could at most abandon the government of the country. Maire's grandmother, though she admired Thiers, remained faithful to the Comte de Chambord; his mother to Boulanger; his father believed in some compromise between Napoleon III and Déroulède. Another academic and contemporary of Maire, also from the provinces—Henri de Gaulle—became dean of studies at the Jesuit College of the Immaculate Conception, and brought up *his* children in the same tradition, with the same kind of anxious pride for France and for the symbols of her glory.

The children of such parents (and of many others) did not suffer only from the evident break between the principles they imbibed at home and those which held good in *La Foire sur la Place;* they resented the difference between the values they were taught at school and the professional or social activity that followed on their studies. Society was turning democratic, but higher education remained elitist. And, while the graduates and *agrégrés* were invited to join the elite, the socio-economic conditions they were offered failed to match either promises or claims of their superiority. Lycées and faculties produced more intellectuals than a stagnant economy could absorb; the excess had to be accommodated in cafés, *cénacles* and *petites revues*, at least pending adjustments. It is not surprising that many denounced the divorce between reality and sanctimonious fictions, and that many more lent them a ready ear.

But here the story becomes complicated. The "society," the power elite of an earlier day, lived on and kept its economic and, hence, its social power, even while political power was slipping from its grasp. In this break between political and social power (between the 5th and the 7th arrondissement, or the 6th and the 16th) lies one factor of the confusion that marks the whole Third Republic. For, while criticisms of the old order fused from the very midst of "society" itself, criticism of its economic basis never did. The critics of cultural and social values never touched the ground in which those values were rooted, the firm economic foundations of the pillars of society they fustigated with their scorn. How could they, when the economic facts were largely responsible for their own existence? Why should they, when ethical and aesthetical considerations offered the most tempting of alternatives?

From this point of view, the tumult and the shouting of our two decades seems a diversion from a reality too harsh for some, too convenient for others. Even anti-Semitism (as I have tried to show in my recent writings) appears in this guise as a brilliant move to channel economic resentments away from hard facts to a conveniently irrelevant scapegoat. And literature itself seems to mirror other interests: political, economic. It is a striking fact that *Le Roman russe* and *L'Emprunt russe* are pretty much coeval, the first dating from 1886, the second from 1888; and that the popularity of Russian literature owes something to publicity campaigns inspired by sadly material reasons. Similarly, one wonders how far Barrès's literary nationalism reflects the economic nationalism of its time, how far the cultural protectionism that Barrès's 1892 exclusion of alien influences reflects maybe the counterpart of Méline's famous tariff of the same year, itself the culmination of a series of measures prompted by agricultural and industrial depression. Faced with falling agricultural prices, cheaper industrial goods from abroad, awkward alien ideas, all could agree that foreign competition called for higher protective walls. The ivory tower in which a young aesthete had once sought refuge from barbarians was refurbished to stand the foreign siege. It was a triumph of the lazy spirit which hid equally behind the periphrases of most *littérateurs*, politicians, or financial spokesmen.

Yet all this is unfair. Such coincidences may be significant; they are not deliberate. The charge to bring against the intellectuals of this time, whether on the *Tâches d'encre* or *Le Semeur,* is not one of devious hypocrisy but of complacency and laziness. While they insisted on pressing their investigations below the surface of perception, they failed to dig as deep below the surface of society. Indeed, their researches in the one direction seem to have dispensed them from going very far in the other. Economics they dismissed as irrelevant, and so it was to them. But, oddly enough, contemporary Socialists seem to have thought so, too.

The originality of the Marxian point of view is its subordination of ideological, intellectual, even political questions to economic ones, its treatment of moral or political interpretations as delusions, its definition of political or cultural developments as epiphenomena on the surface of true reality. We can see how this approach would suit the tendency of the time. Yet, leaving aside a few, and hardly-noticed, people, the Marxian impression upon the *fin de siècle* was negligible. When Rolland turned to socialism, it was to find in it an aliment for the soul. For Péguy, "La Révolution sociale sera morale, ou elle ne sera pas." For Anatole France, socialism was a "new religion," to be surveyed with charitable scepticism. For Zola it was a kind of romantic biology. Even for a syndicalist leader, what counted was "the *élan,* the revolutionary attitude, the aggressive vigor," of the workers. No wonder that another Socialist would deplore "the stupefying indifference of most French workers towards economic organization," and their habit of "expecting the end of all their troubles from political action."[35]

What many amateurs appreciated in socialism, was the spur it applied to their imagination. The great socialist tribunes of this time were humanists and rhetoricians like Viviani, like Jaurès, for whom socialism had partly abolished the frontier between dream and reality, and suggested more possibilities in the latter than current ideas had been able to envisage. A means of salvation, a poetry of action, a kind of surrealism, eventually a deliberate myth: such is the image of *fin de siècle* socialism.

This being so, socialism was drawn into political and cultural entanglements from which it could and perhaps should have remained detached. It was because the lead of socialist movements was taken by middle class intellectuals, with the middle class values and vision of the society they were supposed to oppose, that French socialism enrolled itself in categories and conflicts whose reality it actually denies (like Left and Right; or, in the Dreyfus case, the justice or injustice of bourgeois courts). But this was possible only because the socialist troops themselves accepted the values, shared the vision of the middle-class intellectuals who led or indoctrinated them. And this was partly due to the education the workers received, not only in state schools, but also in popular universities which saw their brief heyday during these years; and to a new socio-economic mobility, opportunity (higher real wages, scholarships, social promotion) that seemed to justify the leaders' insistence on political issues alien to the fundamental insights and preoccupations of socialism.

The new mobility, the improved living standards, confirmed the belief that the decisions of men, their reasoned actions, could actually change society. One result of this was that just when Marxism was catching on with the workers, the development of their condition ceased to bear out the laws of capitalism as Marx described them. Hence, as Marxism spread, dissensions and divisions spread with it in socialist movements which tried to reconcile reality, doctrine, and action, and which succeeded only in relegating them behind the appeals of social romanticism.

The misadventure of dedicated Socialists furnishes the alibi of the dilettantes. Cultural reform was a social question, for culture reflected and affected the society in which it withered or thrived. Social reform meant political reform, and political reform had proved its effectiveness in 1877, in 1879, and in a whole series of admirable measures, each one evoked by another date. If the political panacea faltered, corruption was the cause, attested by the resignation of a President whose son-in-law sold nominations to the Legion-of-Honor to the highest bidder, by the names of ministers and deputies on the counterfoils of lobbyists' checkbooks, by the "syndicates" reputedly attempting to buy or to discredit soldiers and magistrates and clerics, by the old-boy network around the public trough.

An earlier day might have trusted in God or Progress to put things right. But in the eighties the doctrine of social responsibility and the proof of political possibility converged to supersede the easier determinism of yore. People were called upon to do something and they were told that what they did could be effective. What could they do? They were not going to upset a social order which went well enough. They would "found a publication." They would declare that every article, every work of art is an action. It is a sobering thought that Sartre's doctrine of today was launched upon the readers of the *Nouvelle Revue* by Bourget in 1881.[36] They would identify theory with practice and, in their theories, insist on the corrupt core of a society whose politics, morals, and culture were all vitiated by this ever-more-evident flaw. The energies of intellectuals were turned to moral campaigns, the moral campaigns devoted to heightening energy, the cult of energy led almost inevitably to the disparagement of intellectual values.

As the nineties drew to an end, the questing eclecticism of the previous decade had hardened into pragmatic dogmas. The political struggles of the years from Boulanger to Dreyfus had done their share to ensure this. The economic expansion that preceded the war was to encourage it. A newly positive period approved of positive ideas. Positions hardened. The Socialists rediscovered (or discovered at last) a historical determinism in which the *freiwillig* politics of free enterprise gave way to the duty of carrying out one's historical and social mission. Their opponents did the same. Rebelling against the growing power and impersonality of modern capital (which nineteenth century France had long ignored, exaggerating the power and importance of family concerns), the insurgency of traditional forces would be confused with the social and economic demands of the new socialism. Syndicalists and integral nationalists would occasionally join forces. Revolution and reaction would both oppose the established order. But all would speak a language foreign to Jean Barois, as it was to Péguy and Romain Rolland. Only Bourget could feel at home in it, as a repentant and reactionary determinist. And Barrès, whose cult of the Self had been extended to the nation, found that his plea for energy furnished the dominant theme of the nationalist revival.

Either of the hostile young students whom Barois interviewed in 1913 could have contributed to Agathon's famous inquiry, *Les Jeunes Gens d'aujourd'hui,* whose subtitle reads: "The Taste for Action." Both may have applauded Maurice Donnay's latest play, *Les Eclaireuses*, whose hero laughs at a girl for her dated ideas: "I recognize them. . . . I have had them all between twenty-five and thirty, like most men of my generation. Yes, I have been a demolisher and, as for idle nonsense, I did not miss a trick. . . . But lately I have made my choice."

Choice: *voilà le grand mot lâché!* It had been possible to lounge, to loaf, to linger, to taste and try a little of this or that, to squander time and energy and sometimes talent, to be capricious, erratic, and perverse. That was *la belle époque*, when, for Péguy's "everybody," nothing really pressed. And then the clouds gathered, the wheels began to turn, the cost of living became higher, the lower orders less deferent, whims less amusing, fatuousness less fashionable, and one grew old. Even young men grew older. They chose sooner, and that restricted choice. The cult of Self had borne its fruits, and Jean Barois was dying.

The Tortoise and the Hare

A Study of Valéry, Freud, and Leonardo da Vinci

by Roger Shattuck

In Bertrand Russell's *Wisdom of the West,* one comes upon two superbly chosen illustrations on facing pages. On the left Marie Curie stands erect in her austere laboratory, waiting to resume work with her electrical equipment. On the right Sarah Bernhardt poses amid the bric-a-brac of her histrionic sensibility, her handsome head tilted in an expression of infinite longing and infinite boredom. We chuckle over the neatness of the juxtaposition and comprehend the opposition it represents of two sensibilities, two ways of reckoning with life. The history of this split has not yet been written. St. Paul and St. Augustine and St. Thomas Aquinas all distinguish three orders of being: body, mind, and spirit. Descartes reduces the three to two: body and mind, in almost total separation. It was Pascal who reopened a subtle fissure in the midst of thought by distinguishing between *l'esprit de géométrie* and *l'esprit de finesse*—an untranslatable distinction not at all clear in his work but long remembered nevertheless.

The eighteenth century sailed along seemingly unperturbed by the fact that things might be coming apart, and then the nineteenth century seriously took up the task of dividing the human mind into opposing faculties. Cartesian rationalism congealed into positivist theory with its idea of science and history as a growing collection of facts that would reveal their own significance in the shape of law and order. Professor Henry Morgenau makes the point about positivism in a lucid article, "The New Style of Science." "Science, then, according to this pristine understanding, is an aggregate of facts, often of trivia, put together with a suffusion of majesty about their mere factualness." Next to this idea of scientific fact, romanticism spawned a tradition that declared the only true values are feelings—the passions and inner responses that tell us what and how and why we are. Out of this conviction Madame de Staël could write in *De l'Allemagne*: "In effect, when we abandon ourselves completely to reflections, images, and desires that surpass the limits of our experience, then only do we begin to breathe freely." The old conflict between faith and reason gives way to a new conflict about the very faculty with which we should encounter experience: reason or instinct, thought or feeling, intelligence or sensibility. The opposition is attributed shakily to Rousseau, affirmed by Matthew Arnold and Rimbaud and the decadents and D. H. Lawrence, and given social status in the purported alienation of the artist from the bourgeois values of the era.

The two photographs of Marie Curie and Sarah Bernhardt come to stand less for two types of woman than for a division in the mind, a necessary choice between the forces of reason and the forces of feeling. Ample evidence for the division can be mustered. One can hear an army of professors haranguing their classes on the dangers of specialization, the anti-intellectual as a political force, the symptomatic significance of Bergson, and the tragic isolation of the artist in our time. A recent formulation by R.-M. Albérès in the introduction to *L'Aventure intellectuelle du XXe siècle* carries the story down to the present:

> The European sensibility in the twentieth century is characterized by the belief that there exists a divorce between the intelligence on the one hand and, on the other, reality, truth, or instinct. The very term *intelligence* creates a problem, something like what we commonly call a "complex." Before

1860 the question did not arise; neither Voltaire nor Stendhal used the word "intelligence" very often. By a tendency toward self-punishment, perhaps, Europe has created and invented within itself a rending apart of "intelligence."

Such a statement brings us to a crossroads in the forest through which pass Gourmont's "dissociation of sensibility" appropriated by T. S. Eliot, Eric Heller's "disinherited mind," C. P. Snow's two cultures, and a whole flock of images to express the drawing up of frontiers between positivistic science and romantic sensibility during the nineteenth century. A further stage in the separation is sometimes detected around the turn of the century in the form of new discoveries in physics (relativity and quantum theories) and the toppling of the arts into expressionism and nonfigurative modes.

Our two ladies illustrate this great divorce as the *fin de siècle* imagined it. One wonders whether the furniture of history was not also being moved about in order to accommodate the new arrangement. Which great thinkers or artists out of the past were receiving attention? Aristotle? Jesus? Dante? Montaigne? Goethe? All of them, of course; we know no reliable method of measuring esteem so as to ascertain the culture heroes of an era. Yet one of the most elementary means of discovering about whom people were thinking, writing, and reading is to inventory the titles of books published. My investigations have yielded this hard result: between 1869 and 1919, an average of one full-length book per year was published in Europe on the subject of Leonardo da Vinci. (The number excludes the numerous editions of Leonardo's own writings, and also excludes translations and the flood of articles in reviews.) The list of some fifty items includes the following names: Bernard Berenson, Jakob Burckhardt, Pierre Duhem, Sigmund Freud, Arsène Houssaye, Edward MacCurdy, Dmitri Merejkowski, Walter Pater, Péladan, Smiraglia-Scognamiglio, Gabriel Séailles, Edmondo Solmi, Paul Valéry, and Lionello Venturi. If we set aside the institutionalized figure of Jesus, no other human being, historical or imaginary, appears to have received so much systematic and widely disseminated attention from Western culture during the fifty years under scrutiny.

Now here is a raw piece of information to fit into place. But the job is not easy. In most of these writings, and in the books that have continued to appear about him in slightly diminished numbers, Leonardo emerges as the great ambiguous figure of all time. The impression one comes away with is something like a cross between Benvenuto Cellini and St. Francis of Assisi. What was Leonardo's sex life? Was his real preoccupation magic, or science as we know it? Was he the mere creature of his patrons or a great independent mind? Do his notebooks give us the fragments of a supremely organized consciousness or the best efforts of a distraught talent? Does his art serve his science or his science his art? In his restless career and spottily preserved work, should we read triumph or tragedy? I shall not attempt to answer these questions. In the face of so great a bulk of publication on Leonardo, my attention gravitates irresistibly to two books that are the shortest on scholarship yet the most revealing of a particular strain of thinking—in Leonardo's mind, in their authors' minds, and in the climate of an era. The names Paul Valéry and Sigmund Freud stand for two of the most independent, courageous, and productive intelligences of recent times. What they wrote about the great Italian, apparently unaware of each other's work, carries us off on two fruitful expeditions that reach adjoining countries by different routes.

Paul Valéry wrote and published his earliest poems before he was twenty, while still a law student in Montpellier. His mind had been attracted very early to the study of architecture, painting, mathematics, and physics, and to the works of Poe, Huysmans, and Mallarmé. Through the writer Pierre Louys, he came to know Mallarmé, then entering his fifties, and Gide, just Valéry's own age. In 1892 at the age of twenty-three he underwent a kind of conversion in reverse, a period of profound self-doubt leading to a night of turmoil in Genoa. Subsequently he turned away from poetry toward further study in the sciences and history. It was twenty years before he returned to literature with a succession of poems, essays, notes, translations, introductions, and plays that made him the leading poet of France in the thirties and forties. He bore the major responsibility for keeping the French Academy free of taint during the German occupation. His elaborate state funeral in 1945 symbolized the country's resolve, following the liberation, to reaffirm its great intellectual and artistic traditions. Valéry wrote six different texts on Leonardo at approximately even intervals throughout his career. The first two are the most important, *Introduction à la méthode de Léonard de Vinci,* begun in 1894 soon after his detachment from poetry, and *Note et digression,* added to the previous text when it was republished in 1919. In 1929-30 he wrote extensive marginal notes to these two early texts and to a third written in 1928, so that today they appear as a palimpsest, the apt representation of a mind that could endlessly develop and transform any subject just by bringing attention to bear on it.

Valéry opens the *Introduction* by stating flatly that neither the biography nor the personality of Leonardo concerns him. Rather he will examine a method of thinking or a "creature of thought" to whom, because it appears the most appropriate, he assigns the name Leonardo. In prose so dense that one can feel the sustained cerebration that formed it, Valéry describes an elevated, universal, and perpetually self-correcting Mind. Its secret is to grasp "relations . . . between things whose principle of continuity escapes the rest of us." Thus, for both Leonardo and Napoleon, "at the crucial moment they had only to act." This hypersensitive ability to see connections is rendered bearable by a compensatory mechanism of "foresight" that carries every train of thought instantaneously to its limit, a heightened capacity for compression and comparison. Valéry is somewhat hard put to explain the operation of this form of consciousness. What he says about how thought organizes undifferentiated impressions resembles Taine's theory of *hallucination vraie*. He seems to be on firmer ground in considering the two complementary faculties of universal thought: to identify with individual things—a strong sense of particularity in the world—and to recognize regularities in the world: continuity, similarity, periodicity. The truly great mind exercises these faculties at a speed so high as to appear instantaneous, yet remains at least partially conscious of the mental operation taking place within it.

Valéry's reflections (reflexions) on the nature of thought and subjectivity make difficult reading. In a curious way, though Valéry's theory of mind is diametrically opposed to that of biologically-oriented behaviorists and sociologists, what he writes often sounds like an elaborate restatement of the dictum: "Mind is minding." But the cross-hatch and chain-stitch of his style convey Valéry's perpetual refinement of such an equivocation. The pure activity, the mere free play of mind is as exciting and as productive as any externally imposed purpose or special discipline. This in fact is the point with which he begins the later essay, *Note et digression*. He swoops back down on Leonardo as the "leading actor in the intellectual comedy which never to this day has found its poet." In a less clotted, more transparent prose, Valéry reaffirms this judgment of the "integrity" of Leonardo as a mind, never torn between a naturalistic and a spiritualistic sense of man. But another, more subtle division lurks within, for which Valéry offers the expression, "presence of mind." He illustrates the delicate circular equilibrium of this self-awareness with two metaphors: first, the swirling drafts that form a smoke ring, and second, the stage of a theater surrounded by a hidden but distinctly real audience. Finally these two easily grasped figures are plunged together to a deeper level of discourse and of mind:

> The character of man is consciousness; and the character of consciousness is a perpetual emptying, an unremitting unsparing detachment from everything that appears, no matter how it appears. An inexhaustible act independent of the quality or number of things that present themselves, and by

which the *man in the mind* [*l'homme de l'esprit*] must knowingly restrict himself to being an indefinite refusal to be anything at all.

Before this endless self-repulsion of mind, all things are equal. What survives, the pure impersonal self of consciousness, sounds to Valéry like the very bass note of our existence. Leonardo represents this intensified and complex presence of mind, as much the result, Valéry concludes, as the cause of his works.[1]

In these two texts and the later ones, Valéry has composed variations on a single theme: the miraculous variety of Leonardo's work springs from a highly developed singleness of mind or unity of thought. Examined in itself, apart from the works it strewed along its path, this astonishing mind reveals the nature of the self, not personality or biography but pure consciousness beholding an infinity of relations in what it sees and perpetually backing away from what it sees in the very act of beholding.[2]

At the end of the first essay on Leonardo, Valéry quotes a sentence in which, he submits, Leonardo has expressed a purely modern concept:

> The air is full of infinite, straight, radiant lines crossing and interweaving without one ever entering the path of another, and they represent for each object the true FORM of its cause.
> L'aria e piena d'infinite linie rette e radoise insieme intersegate e intessute sanza ochupatione luna dellaltra rapresantano aqualunche obieto lauera forma della lor chagione.

Valéry relates this sentence to the undulatory theory of light, to the old absurdity of "action at a distance" in gravitational theory, and then successively to the work of Faraday, Maxwell, and Lord Kelvin. Remember, this is a disaffected poet aged twenty-three writing in 1894 when the results of the Michelson-Morley experiment six years earlier had not yet gained universal acceptance. He was discovering in Leonardo da Vinci an early formulation of field theory, something that had not yet taken clear shape out of Maxwell's electro-magnetic theory published twenty years before.

Edmund Wilson has pointed out in *Axel's Castle* the evident vanity in Valéry's parading of scientific materials in much of his writing. But here Valéry sums up in one all-encompassing idea the various aspects of consciousness that he has brought out earlier: rigor, continuity, compression, contrast, symmetry, regularity. Himself of course an outstanding example of the mentality he was exploring, Valéry saw the relation between the infinity of visible connections between all things apparent to a supremely attuned imagination like Leonardo's, and the infinity of physical connections between all things soon to be established by field theory. This essay on a Renaissance subject is less historical than prophetic.

The word that chants the refrain in Valéry's series of texts on Leonardo is *continuity*. And in the quoted passage expressing a vast unity of creation, Valéry is expanding and refining into scientific terms the now commonplace doctrine of *correspondences*. Its recent history goes back to Swedenborg, Fourier, Novalis, Blake, Baudelaire, and Yeats. But Valéry made bold to transpose the idea of discontinuous and analogical correspondences, parallels between different things, into the idea of a continuum, a single medium or field displaying modifications that we call "things" yet not separable into different entities. The mind is one in this text as, some ten years later, space and time would be affirmed as one in the special theory of relativity. And Valéry concludes the 1919 text with a reference to the problem of the existence of intelligences outside our own as being "comparable to the physical problem of relativity."

Until 1910 Freud's theory of mind had stressed the division between primary or instinctual thought processes operating according to the pleasure principle, and secondary or inhibitory thought processes observing the reality principle. The last chapter of *The Interpretation of Dreams* gives the best systematic account of the two processes, and one still hears in this text, finished in 1900, the professional neurologist both urging on and cautioning the vigorous young analyst. The chapter in question, once it has established the two thought processes and the areas of consciousness and unconsciousness they rule, pays lengthy attention to the principle that guards the frontier: repression or censorship. Gradually, however, Freud shifted his attention from separation to communication between these areas. The last of the Clark lectures, delivered in 1909, contains at its close a fine paragraph that recognizes the previously little-mentioned process of sublimation as psychically and socially valuable. "It is probable that we owe our highest cultural successes to the contributions of energy made in this way to our mental processes." Within a few months Freud began work on Leonardo.

Freud was over fifty when he wrote his first and only psychoanalytic biography. The subject was not new to him. "Perhaps the most famous left-handed individual was Leonardo," he had written in a letter in 1898, "who is not known to have had any love affairs." A questionnaire in 1907 revealed that Merejkowski's novel, *The Gods Reborn: Leonardo da Vinci,* was one of Freud's favorite books. Then in 1909, right after the Clark lectures, he was consulted by a patient whose temperament strongly resembled that of Leonardo, though without the Italian's genius. Impelled from so many sides toward Leonardo, Freud bought several works on him and began extensive reading. It was only at this point that he discovered the text of Leonardo's remarkable childhood recollection. That brief passage provided the framework for the study entitled *Leonardo da Vinci and a Memory of His Childhood.*

The disclaimer with which Freud begins differs from Valéry's. The fact that he is studying Leonardo, Freud tells us, does not suggest that the great Italian genius was a pathological case, nor even represent any desire to detract from his fame. Freud affirms he is concerned with "laws which govern normal and pathological activity with equal cogency." The problem Freud first poses is the apparent interference that occurred between Leonardo's investigative activities and his painting, between scientist and artist.

The first and longest of the six sections advances the thesis that Leonardo's truly exceptional capacities as an experimental investigator, unimpeded by the authority of either church or antiquity, can be traced in great part to his childhood, through the theory of sublimation. "After his curiosity had been aroused in infancy, he succeeded in sublimating the greater part of his libido into an urge for research." His notes and his behavior show that he felt compelled "to love in such a way as to hold back the affect, subject it to the process of reflection." This instinct for knowledge, though it channeled his genius, in the end affected the free play of his artistic expression. What was left of his childhood sexuality, Freud supposes, expressed itself as sublimated homosexuality.

The remaining pages flesh out this hypothesis with a brilliant, though often factually unsupported, demonstration. Freud quotes from a German translation the famous sentence from the *Codex Atlanticus* given by Scognamiglio:

> It seems I was always destined to be so deeply concerned with vultures; for I recall as one of my very earliest memories that while I was in my cradle a vulture came down to me, and opened my mouth with its tail, and struck me many times with its tail against my lips.

Freud interprets it as a passive homosexual phantasy of fellatio transferred to infantile suckling. Unfortunately "vulture" is a mistranslation of *nibio,* which means kite; part of Freud's more elaborate bird and mother symbolism collapses as a result. He reconstructs a plausible but unprovable portrait of the illegitimate infant Leonardo alone with his doting mother and then adopted by his father, married but as yet without legitimate children. In his father's prosperous household Leonardo was further indulged. These pages give one of the earliest discussions of the origins of homosexuality in narcissism: desiring to reinforce his mother's love for him and to identify with it as an extension of his self-love, the son indulges his love for her to the point of substituting himself for her, looking for a male partner, and thus remaining faithful to his mother. Freud attributes the mysterious blend of reserve and seductiveness we call "Leonardesque" to the painter's having been reminded of his mother by the model for the "Mona Lisa." Thenceforward that ambivalent expression characterizes all his female figures, including the two in "Virgin and Child and St. Anne." In that composition Freud detects a recollection of Leonardo's two young mothers, the real and the adopted. After associating Leonardo's great preoccupation with flight—bird flight and human flight—with a throwback to his childhood sexual researches when he was alone with his mother, Freud concludes with a reaffirmation that Leonardo's extreme case of inhibition was not pathological or neurotic but obsessional and healthy. Freud concedes the insufficiency of the material evidence on which to construct a case, the need "to recognize here a degree of freedom" in Leonardo's choice of actions, and the "limits which are set to what psychoanalysis can achieve in the field of biography." Yet he believes that the key to Leonardo's great and mysterious genius lay in his capacity to direct and transmute the deep feelings aroused in him during childhood.

The reservations that have to be made about hanging so much mass of interpretation on a single sentence can be found elsewhere.[3] The passage on which Freud's argument pivots occurs about ten pages after the opening. He states in effect that what might be seen as two separate problems in Leonardo must be interpreted as one:

> There is only one way in which the peculiarity of this emotional and sexual life can be understood in connection with Leonardo's double nature as an artist and as a scientific investigator.

The "one way" means of course sublimation, in this case accompanied by narcissism and homosexuality. But the last two items are far less important than the central hypothesis that in Leonardo we witness a mind that succeeds in defending its integrity and defeats the censor, even if at some final cost in dispersion of talent.

This would seem a long way to come if these two highly individual books have little in common but their subject and their total inadequacy as systematic biographies. But the reason for the comparison should begin to assert itself. Valéry, whom we think of as an artist, gives most of his attention to Leonardo's notebooks and to his methodology as a thinker. Freud, whom we think of as a scientist, at least by training, refers briefly to the notebooks and then elaborates the greater part of his argument on the basis of the painting and the life. Valéry cites no historical persons, dates, or places, and attempts only to illustrate a theory of self-consciousness; Freud obviously believed he could contribute to Leonardo's biography and to biographical method by bringing to bear on an enigmatic and eminent life the new science of analysis. Yet by the time we reach the end of Freud's study, Leonardo's personality interests us less than the process that permitted him to come to terms with himself and the world. Not the individuality but the generality of his case emerges from these pages. His personality has melted away into a set of carefully described responses.

Why, then, if neither author wrote a biography but was really concerned with something quite apart from Leonardo's individual life, did they compose these two books nominally aimed in his direction? The first answer is quite easy. They both identified with Leonardo—admired him, understood something of him, and could understand something of themselves in examining him. Though Valéry's first article was commissioned, the subject was far from new to him. He makes little effort to hide the fact that what he writes of Leonardo is in effect the fruit of introspection. And he wrote at far greater length on Leonardo than on any other person, including his master Mallarmé. Freud's interest in Leonardo went back at least a dozen years and probably more, and the work remained one of his favorites. Ernest Jones tells us that Freud particularly admired two historical figures: Moses, the wise leader who guided his people to a new land and a full life, and Leonardo, who combined the talents of an artist and the knowledge of a scientist in creating some of the greatest artifacts of Western culture. There is nothing very rash in saying that both Valéry and Freud felt in themselves the double temperament, the twin genius that tradition attributes to Leonardo. Furthermore Leonardo's apparent irresolution and perpetual shift of focus in his work probably struck a responsive cord in each of them. Valéry had just gone through a personal crisis that was to divert the channel of his writing for many years: he came to value a completed work less than the state of mind that permits creation. Freud, though well established in his central field of inquiry when he wrote on Leonardo, had been very much at loose ends for a time about what calling to follow. After deciding against law, a slow and somewhat erratic progress had carried him through physiology, medicine, teaching, neurology, and psychopathology to psychoanalysis. He was always profoundly attracted to literature and the arts, and wrote to the novelist Stifter that he felt their temperaments were very similar.

But more important than any personal reasons for writing of Leonardo, the conclusions of their studies show more similarity than we might have expected. I have suggested earlier that the books contribute to a discernible pattern that reveals Leonardo as a culture hero for the era. Yet these two works, weak as they are biographically, help us understand why so many other authors were studying Leonardo without shedding much new light. From their very different cultural vantage points, Valéry and Freud glimpsed something behind Leonardo they could approach through him. For both of them, Leonardo stood for a form of consciousness they admired—a new equilibrium of faculties that could be fully recognized and appreciated only four hundred years after the fact and on slender evidence. Their essays describe a case that has particular relevance to our modern situation, like Eliot writing of Donne, or Baudelaire writing of Poe. I feel that in the end, for Freud as much as for Valéry, the name Leonardo is reduced to an exemplary case, a convention, a pure symbol, a term like "Socrates" as traditionally used in the syllogisms that start "Socrates is a man." Someone has to represent humanity, if possible at its best. But subtracted from his life, what does Leonardo stand for? Does anything remain beyond Vasari's appealing myth of a restless genius releasing birds, blowing up bladders, and painting an occasional picture?

Three semi-parenthetical remarks will clear the ground a little around these questions. To begin with, Valéry's *Note et digression* carries one of the most merciless and concise attacks on Pascal (his name is not mentioned in the text) that has ever been composed. It is too good to miss:

> [Leonardo] had not the least knowledge of that gross and ill-defined opposition which, a century and a half later, was declared between *l'esprit de finesse* and *l'esprit de géométrie* by a man entirely insensible to the arts, who could not conceive of that natural but delicate blending of talents. It was he who lured us into a wager that gobbled up all finesse and all geometry, and who, having changed his new lamp for an old one, wasted his time sewing little notes into his pockets, when the moment had come to bring to France the glory of having discovered infinitesimal calculus. . . .

No, Leonardo was not wasting his time on dividing the mind against itself and setting odds on immortality. The passage is significant. Secondly, nothing in Freud's analysis of Leonardo's tendency to abandon his painting for elaborate, fragmentary, and often mysterious scientific studies inclines in the slightest toward the concept of schizophrenia. On the contrary, this double man, distracted as he may have appeared on the outside, incapable of finishing much of what he started, and careless of the fate of what he did finish, exemplified a high level of inner integration. "Our aim remains that of demonstrating the connection along the path of instinctual activity between a person's external experiences and his reactions." Here at the end of the essay Freud affirms for the second time that Leonardo made these connections very well indeed.

The last remark concerns the French mathematician Poincaré, who began publishing in the nineties a series of articles on the intuitive, unconscious nature of mathematical imagination, on the distinction between fact and hypothesis, and on the significance of the new physics. Though these writings found a large audience only when they appeared in book form (1902-09), Valéry read the articles as they appeared, consulted Poincaré personally on a mathematical point, and cited him for support in the first text on Leonardo. A year later Valéry wrote André Gide that he was thinking of composing a literary portrait of the mathematician. "Poincaré is hard to do without knowing the man. He interests me very much, for he hardly does anything now but psychological articles on mathematics. That's exactly to my taste." And he regrets not knowing Poincaré well. Evidently the "novel" about an imaginary personage, *Monsieur Teste,* the *Introduction* to the hypothetical mind of Leonardo, and the unwritten study of the contemporary mathematician turned psychologist all represent one preoccupation, in effect one work. We discover also that Freud received from Maria Bonaparte a copy of Poincaré's *La Valeur de la science* (1905), a book which he read with interest and sympathy because it corroborated his conviction that science could never replace religion. Science teaches not to have faith but to doubt the things about which we feel most certain. Freud's letter to Maria Bonaparte makes it clear that psychoanalysis had particular reasons to keep its doubts about itself.

Valéry's attack on Pascal's irresponsible dividing of the mind into two parts, Freud's reluctance to see Leonardo as a man at odds with his own most precious talents, and their common interest in Poincaré's psychology of scientific and creative thinking—these circumstances reinforce what should already be clear about the coincidence that Valéry and Freud both wrote about an Italian painter and thinker who lived four hundred years before their time. They did not see in him a universal genius who represents the variety of human faculties vying with each other in a great divergence of roles and activities. His versatility led them in another direction. Their two highly contrasting books relentlessly trace the multiplicity and contradiction of Leonardo's activities back to a mind. And above all, that mind is one, an integrity of scientist and artist, of sensibility and intelligence. All Valéry's terms (method, invention, central attitude, presence of mind) grant to that master mind a tremendous freedom to see from a single vantage point the continuity of all things around it.[4] Freud's elaborate apparatus for describing two cities in the mind (or three, if one counts the preconscious along with the conscious and unconscious) gradually vanishes as he approaches Leonardo. And the lesson of the book is that a single, all-encompassing power, an incredible integrity of mind, can result from a mingling of previously separated energies. One can distinguish different directions for investigation (sex, science, art), but the "case" of Leonardo displays not different drives or instincts but a single common activity of mind that gives rise to all these.

And thus, along with Pascal, a whole tradition of dualism in the mind comes a cropper if we draw the full conclusion. Valéry did; his precocious certainty about the indivisibility of the mind probably explains the coyness with which he indulges in interdisciplinary by-play in some of his writings. But his vision was steady. Freud unfortunately never tested his theories against another mind equal to Leonardo's and turned increasingly to culture and society as his subject. His dualistic terminology has remained, but I maintain that his essay on Leonardo lets us see how strongly Freud felt drawn toward an interpretation of mental activity as one, only artificially divisible. At the very moment when, we are usually told, Western consciousness was hardening into a division between reason and feeling, two of the greatest contemporary minds were saying precisely the opposite in terms that recapitulate the history of modern European thought. They assert, in effect, that the experience of four hundreds years tells us urgently and insistently not to divide up the mind. For to oppose one faculty to another implies that the drift toward specialization has its source in our thinking, a kind of racism of the mind prone to segregation. Furthermore they avoid the error of Vico and Comte and finally Lévy-Bruhl, who affirmed the existence of primitive thought as an essentially different functioning of mind from our civilized thought.[5] No one has ever satisfactorily demonstrated that the "savage" makes associations and forms conclusions about his animistic or god-ridden world any differently than we do. Nor —to take an extreme example—need the "logic" of Rimbaud's *Les Illuminations,* or of *Alice in Wonderland,* or of a nightmare, by any different from the "logic" that should be connecting one proposition to another on this page.

Valéry and Freud do not indulge in any suggestion that the superiority of Leonardo's mental organization, his power to perceive relations and find pleasure in experiment, removed him from humanity. On the contrary, an image they both use displays their awareness of the risks run by so powerful a mind if aware of its own power. Valéry's exposition never withdraws from the dilemma of self-consciousness, so that every metaphor for thought or attention ("the dream of the waking sleeper," "detachment," "repulsion") signifies a perpetual spiraling out of the self in order to see the self—which is no longer there to be seen. Throughout his poetic production, Valéry reverted to the figure of Narcissus to express this problem of the fugitive self: and narcissism is precisely the psychoanalytic concept to which Freud gave one of its earliest elaborations in the Leonardo text. The metaphor does not serve the same purpose for the two of them; but in both cases its meaning reaches far into the ambiguous area where the mind, trying to catch sight of itself in action, discovers that nothing is there but a perpetual movement of recoil or afterthought. Narcissus attests not to a division but to a contortion of mind. Freud points out very shrewdly that nothing seemed to escape the notice of Leonardo's investigations. "Yet his urge for knowledge was always directed to the external world; something kept him far away from the investigation of the human mind. . . . There was little room for psychology." In other words, Leonardo would never have written either Valéry's or Freud's book.

So limited a demonstration as this could never "prove" that all thought is one. Nor could it hope to flatten the barriers that have grown up between a long series of artificial opposites, not the least of which is the inseparable pair: theory-fact. And even if the theory-fact of the unity of thought is accepted as demonstrated in the specific instances of Valéry and Freud looking at Leonardo, the problem remains of why we cling to different words for such versions as patient observation, discursive logic, intuition, a flash of inspiration, reverie, and the like. Or more specifically, how is it Freud associates wit-work, dream-work, and artistic creation and treats that cluster of activities as distinguishable from the thought patterns that direct our ordinary living? And then there is the even more troubling question of why certain forms of presumably rational thought, such as the implications of quantum and relativity theory, or theories about time and entropy, bear a close resemblance to their decreed opposites, dream and fantasy. The answer, I believe, lies close at hand in the pacing of mental events. Both Freud and Valéry speak of rapidity and compression.

Our thinking, in a manner no one has yet described satisfactorily to my knowledge, has a widely variable speed. The same operations of association and dissociation take place slowly in activities we refer to as "reasoning it out" or "systematic analysis," and with infinitely greater speed in dream and hunch and wit. However, it is ridiculous to assume—as we usually do—that our minds work at a nearly uniform rate in any given interval. Inspiration or intuition comes in the midst of the dullest analysis. The dross that surrounds the vividness of a remembered dream probably just goes unrecorded. In the superb essay, *Mathematical Invention,* Poincaré describes how he discovered Fuchsian functions not during the long hours spent sitting at his work table but one morning as he was stepping into a bus. It sounds like a page out of Proust. Nevertheless those seemingly fruitless hours were necessary, for the solutions they eliminated and for the inner expectancy they built up. Valéry decribes the composition of his poem, "La Cimetière marin," in the same fashion. Scientists or poets, we do not know the very timing of our minds.

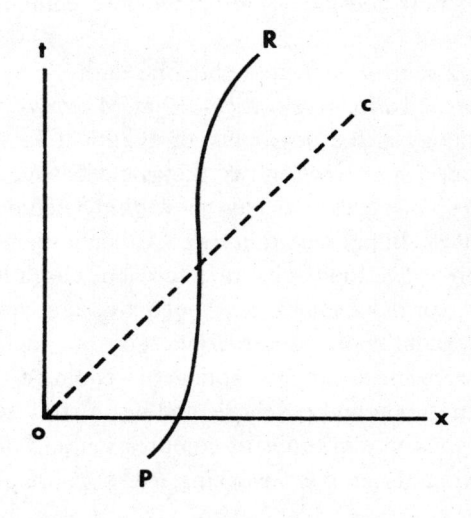

Reasoning by analogy is a very dangerous procedure. Yet the experimenter as much as the artist proceeds on faith—the faith that his mind can truly come to terms with reality and that there is always a higher order of things for him to discover. (That faith is often called doubt.) I wish to argue from one of the most ambitious theories of orderliness in nature back into the jungle of the mind. Einstein's special theory of relativity was given graphical expression almost immediately by Minkowski, whose four-dimensional geometry does an enormously helpful job of representing physical reality. In the figure below, the x axis represents the three dimensions of space and t axis represents time measured by a free (i.e. unaccelerated) observer at O. In this geometry a diagonal OC separates time-like curves (more vertical than horizontal) from space-like curves (more horizontal than vertical) and this diagonal represents energy moving at the speed of light, c.

The world line of a single particle, say PR, must be time-like, and as it approaches the limiting speed of light it contracts so enormously as to cease to have the properties of matter. To "jump" into the diagonal it would have to change from matter into energy, according to Einstein's formula, $E = mc^2$. A space-like curve is really a map of points in space which cannot be reached by any one particle's world line. In the xt plane, called space-time or Minkowski space, the velocity of light c is of crucial importance and is assigned some very special characteristics. For example, the world line of energy traveling with this velocity has zero length and is perpendicular to itself. But the significant point is that all this represents a single space, a *continuum,* both connected and articulated by the mysterious diagonal $x = t$ or c. The "light" that travels with unalterable speed is the most commonplace and miraculous element in our environment. What "travels" in time or "stays put" in space is one, energy or mass, according to how you look at it or, more revealingly, according to its velocity.

So it is, I submit, with thought: one entity, one faculty, one process. But of various velocities. What Minkowski space suggests by analogy is the possibility of a critical velocity. In this idea of a frontier not between two things but between two speeds or two states, I suggest we have a working definition of consciousness itself. Below a certain speed, thought seems observable and its coherence verifiable; its trajectory lends itself to expression in discursive forms of language. Above a certain speed, thought outruns any continuous observation, appears incoherent, and finds expression in extremely elliptical or disjointed forms. When he dealt with dream and psychosis and wit, Freud described this high-velocity activity in terms of compression and displacement. They are probably as good working terms as we shall have in some time.

I do not wish to imply a fixed constant of consciousness for all individuals at all times, in the fashion that the constant velocity of light has turned out to be the Rock of Ages in physics. All of us have direct experience of the fluctuations in our own consciousness according to physical and psychical states. Inevitably I am speaking out of my own experience, remembering those exalted yet awkward moments of stumbling onto a mountain-top in the mind from which one beholds the majesty of everything properly in place. In particular, one evening while reading an article on physics after an exhausting day, I suddenly felt an almost physical release within me. Flanked by others I did not recognize, two images flashed vividly into my mind: an early cubist painting by Braque I had seen several months earlier, and the haunting mystery of Poe's stories read many years earlier. And it all came clear. The necessity of anti-matter, the necessity of mirror symmetry, the necessity of the psycho-literary myth of the double, and above all the necessity of myself seeing it thus—all that literally struck me, at once and as one. I found no words to record the blow then; it seemed miraculous yet very familiar, as if I had known it for a long time. Still, the ceiling of consciousness had to lift in order for me to glimpse it. What lures mankind into experimentation with drugs is probably not a direct sensual pleasure but the fact that they can raise (or lower) the critical velocity below which our mental processes reveal themselves. Slow motion effects, geometric music, massive coilings and uncoilings—these drug experiences show the mind, rather than the cosmos, laid bare. Censorship and repression, the processes so roundly criticized by Sartre, could be decribed anew as measurements of distance and the velocity of thought rather than as a separate faculty. Of course just as Minkowski geometry, like any representation of space-time, must include a location for the hypothetical observer, so a representation of consciousness leaves us in the quandary of showing an observer, an *"I"* beholding the trajectory of my own thought. This duality in identity is vastly more real and significant than the false one we started with between intellect and sensibility.

For one very elementary lesson, then, we may look back a medium range of sixty-odd years to the turn of the century. Amid the surprisingly large number of writers in Europe devoting their attention to Leonardo da Vinci, two thinkers discovered the opportunity to approach the most universal subject of all: the nature of the human mind. A little distance beyond the place where their explicit commentary stopped, one can discern a significant agreement. The division we have begun to lament publicly between two climates of thinking, scientific and humanistic, between opposed methods of inquiry, cannot be traced to any corresponding division between regions or faculties in the mind. At the origin is unity; we have imposed the separation upon ourselves, possibly to lighten our burden. For it is an onerous responsibility to live both inside and alongside the thoughts that we are—almost.

There is more than we ever knew in the story of the tortoise and the hare. Just look again. You will see not two animals but one, traveling at different speeds.

Friedrich Meinecke
Historian of a World in Crisis

by Gerhard Masur

During the early years of the nineteenth century German historiography occupied a position of undisputed leadership. Niebuhr, Ranke, and Mommsen set the pace for many a European historian. This position was lost, however, when German historians succumbed to the passion of nationalism. The works of Droysen, Sybel, and Treitschke were no longer inspired by the universal vistas that had moved the older generation. Germany's most significant contributions to the humanities between the years of 1890 and 1914 were made in the field of sociology. The names of Max and Alfred Weber, of Werner Sombart and Georg Simmel, of Ernst Troeltsch and Ferdinand Tönnies come to mind.[1] It is true that a so-called "Ranke renaissance" occurred during the same period, but most of the historians who professed to be disciples of Ranke were, in reality, paying court to the idol of power. The notable exception is Friedrich Meinecke, who traveled the "arduous road from traditionalist nationalism to humanistic cosmopolitanism."[2] His work may, therefore, be considered as symptomatic of various changes which took place in the humanities before and after World War I.

In Meinecke's first significant work he showed himself to be conscious of a singular calling. He wrote: "It may be permitted a younger generation, groaning under the burden of social problems which seem almost insoluble, to turn with a feeling of nostalgia toward those luminous thoughts of the age of the reforms [1807-13], an age in which the state and the ideal of humanity were conjoined and every class was offered the full opportunity to live fully its own life, giving and receiving, learning and teaching. Luminous, eternal thoughts, however much conditioned by the time."[3] The quotation gives evidence of the perennial crisis in which Meinecke spent most of his life, a crisis produced by the rift between the state and the spirit. His was a long life, lasting from 1862 to 1954. He saw the rise of the second German Empire in 1871 and its fall in 1918, and with horror witnessed the rise and fall of the Third Reich. This abundance of historical events sharpened his conceptions, which he corrected at every turn. In the framework of these happenings, Meinecke formulated his history of ideas toward a more mature discipline than the one first conceived by Dilthey; he followed the philosophy of historicism which Croce and Troeltsch had outlined to its conclusion. Last but not least, he aimed at and achieved a synthesis of historical thought and political action which made him one of the outstanding examples of Germany's return to democracy after the debacle of 1945.

Meinecke was born in Salzwedel, a small town in the Mark Brandenburg, but during his early years the family moved to Berlin, and it was here, as a member of a solid middle-class society and in the sober setting of the Prussian capital, that Meinecke was educated. His background was mellowed by the last waves of Lutheran pietism and German romanticism which permeated the parental home.[4] He was eight years old when Bismarck engaged in the Franco-Prussian War which culminated in the foundation of a unified Germany. Like most of his generation, Meinecke fell under Bismarck's spell; the personality of this master diplomat appealed to him, as did the new ideology of *Realpolitik*. With Bismarck and through Bismarck, the Prussian state with its sense of discipline, courage, and sacrifice became one of the important influences of his growing years. But the part of Germany embodied in Potsdam was only one of the elements of his growth.[5]

The other was the classical liberalism and humanism of German literature and philosophy, of her poetry and music: Herder, Humboldt, Schiller, Goethe, Beethoven, and the romantic masters. Thus it was that he came to dedicate himself to the two poles of German life. He did not then anticipate any conflict that might arise from the combination of these two wellsprings of his youth.[6] They had one characteristic in common: they were based on a hierarchy of values and personalities; they were aristocratic and selective. Until very late in life Meinecke adhered to the conviction that the clue to the mystery of the historic process is to be found in great personalities rather than in the masses. The history of ideas inaugurated by Meinecke is based on the intellectual history of great individuals.

Meinecke must have had an early perception of his vocation. He entered the University of Berlin determined to become a historian. He was initiated into the techniques of historical methodology which Leopold Ranke and the historical school had developed to perfection. Meinecke accepted not only their methods but also their general philosophy, which looked upon the conflicts between the great powers as the proper subject for the historian. Meinecke himself has reported that he was deeply impressed by Droysen's lectures. But he also attended the lectures of Dilthey who put the emphasis on the *Geisteswissenschaften*, a seed soon to break ground in Meinecke's own endeavors. Sybel and Treitschke also attracted his burgeoning interests.

At the completion of his studies Meinecke chose the career of the archivist. Throughout his life he suffered from a speech defect, and at the time he believed that the role of the academic teacher was closed to him. For many years he worked in the Prussian archives and felt quite at home in "this dusty trade." Among his fellow archivists was Otto Hintze, destined to become one of the masters of comparative history. He exercised considerable influence on Meinecke. Although Meinecke was shy and reticent by nature, his gifts were soon to be recognized. He was invited to become the editor-in-chief of the *Historische Zeitschrift,* Germany's most important historical review. He retained the editorship until 1935, a position which allowed him considerable influence on historical studies in Germany.

It was during his services in the Prussian archives that Meinecke first reached forth into the world of political ideas. Wilhelm von Humboldt's *Essay on the Tasks of the Historian* encouraged him to strike out on his own. His program for an intellectual history reads as follows: "Ideas, carried and transformed by individual personalities, [form] the canvas of historical life."[7] His own research led him into the political philosophy of the Restoration period. He put his conviction to a further test when he began the biography of Hermann von Boyen, the Prussian minister of war who, in 1814, introduced military conscription in Prussia. Boyen was one of the outstanding liberals of the era of reform, during which so many attempts were made to soften the hardened shell of Prussian monarchy by an infusion of liberal ideas stemming from the French Revolution. The biography of Boyen centers around a problem with which Meinecke would wrestle throughout his life: the union of power and morals, or, as he liked to call it, the union of ethos and kratos. In this book Meinecke showed himself a master of historical analysis, as well as of historical presentation, in his method of describing the technical reorganization of the Prussian army as motivated by the idealistic thought of the age of the reform. "Here military history is transformed into the history of ethical ideals."[8] It was the first proof of the fruitfulness of intellectual history applied to a core of hard and arid facts.

Meinecke's biography of Boyen gave the marshall his proper niche in the history of the nineteenth century. To Meinecke it brought a reputation as one of the promising talents in Germany's academic world. In spite of his scruples and the many doubts he had entertained concerning his fitness as an academic teacher, he found himelf appointed professor of modern European history at the University of Strasbourg.

With Meinecke's move into the southwestern corner of Germany, there came a ripening of his talent which brought his sensitive nature to full bloom. Southwest Germany was then the home of some of the finest minds of the era. The philosophers Rickert and Husserl, the theologian Troeltsch, the sociologist Max Weber, were only some of the men with whom Meinecke came in contact. Besides there were hiking trips along the Rhine and journeys to nearby Switzerland and Italy, activities that gave an added warmth and pleasure to his new life. One of Meinecke's important characteristics was his capacity for growth. He constantly strove to overcome the limitations of his own personality. From rather narrow beginnings he reached out into wider horizons until he finally achieved a truly universal outlook. First in Strasbourg and later from 1908 in Freiburg, he succeeded in shedding the major part of his Prussian parochialism.

For more than a decade Meinecke continued to be fascinated by the problems and paradoxes of German history during the nineteenth century. But it soon became apparent that he was not merely the student of Ranke and Treitschke. In his next work, *Weltbürgertum und Nationalstaat (From Cosmopolitanism to the Nation-state)*, he endeavored to show how cosmopolitanism and nationalism had become deeply intertwined in the development of nineteenth century Germany. Meinecke traced the philosophical and literary origins of the ideology of the nation-state in Germany and soon found himself beyond the borderlines of political history, strictly speaking. He delved into the world of Friedrich Schlegel, Novalis, Fichte, and Hegel to learn where German nationalism was rooted as opposed to the sources of French nationalism. The volume in which he presented his findings was immediately recognized as a masterpiece, the biography of two ideas. Thus he became the historian of political ideas par excellence, a historian of problems rather than the narrator of epic themes after the style of Ranke or Michelet, or the analyst of institutions, like Tocqueville. In setting up the history of political ideas as an independent discipline, Meinecke developed a unique style—subtle, sensitive, and highly expressive of the countless variations and mutations which political ideas produce in their unfolding. He was a pioneer in a hitherto little-explored territory, but he was soon to be followed by such eminent minds as Croce, Cassirer, and Hazard. Meinecke was at his best when pointing out the contrasting poles between which our Western world has moved in its restless evolution: rule and freedom, nationalism and cosmopolitanism, power and ethics, causalities and values, uniqueness and recurrence. This dualism in Meinecke's thinking is perhaps indicative of a cleavage in his nature.[9]

In this manner Meinecke became the founder of a new school of historical thought and moved easily into the frontline of Germany's historians. He gathered around him a number of promising talents, the first generation of the Meinecke-school; these young men looked to him as an inspiring and uncompromising master. Siegfried Kaehler, Hans Rothfels, Hajo Holborn, Hans Baron, and Dietrich Gerhard are some of the scholars who owe their training to him.

In the years before 1914 Meinecke continued to affirm the idea of the nation-state and its corollary, political power, without reservation. He spoke of Hegel, Ranke, and Bismarck as the great liberators who had freed the German mind from its romantic mists and allowed it to advance into a clear and realistic attitude toward the state.

It was natural that from such premises Meinecke should move into the political arena of party fight and strife. He had shed the conservative tendencies of his youth and had joined the right wing of the liberal movement, the national liberals. He wanted to widen the foundations of the nation-state to the point of including the increasing numbers of the working classes. Like many academic men, he came under the influence of Friedrich Naumann. His initial attempts to reach his goal were timorous and lacking in energy; representative government was affirmed not as an end in itself, but as a means to an end, that of enabling Germany to play her role as a world power. His position was not atypical; it was shared by a large portion of the enlightened German bourgeoisie. An illustrative parallel could be drawn between the political thought of Meinecke and that of Max Weber.[10]

Following the lines that he had traced in *Weltbürgertum und Nationalstaat,* Meinecke devoted his attention to one of the tragic figures in Germany's national development, Joseph Maria von Radowitz.[11] This friend of Friedrich Wilhelm IV constitutes an important link between the early unification movement and Bismarck. He was a romanticist and a Catholic who, in 1849, had tried in vain to solve the German problem. Meinecke wrote a perspicacious study of this contradictory and ill-starred personality which ranks high among the biographies of the lost generation of 1848.[12]

Shortly before the outbreak of World War I Meinecke became professor at the University of Berlin. Like so many Europeans, he had thought the great war "probable but impossible." He contributed a number of booklets to the war literature which the modern reader will hesitate to accept. They are full of nationalistic reasoning, if indeed it may be called reason. The war found Meinecke at first quite unprepared to conceive any vista beyond the horizon of Germany's imperialistic aspirations.[13] Only by slow degrees did it dawn on him that this conflict harbored consequences surpassing by far the results of previous engagements between feuding European powers. In its initial steps the war appeared to be but one more encounter in the long series of contentions between the European nations, a test by fire which might affirm the strength of the young German nation-state. It is well known that Thomas Mann succumbed to a similar illusion. But though Meinecke's first reaction was hasty and unsound, he was not one to rest content on a false premise. As Germany's perspectives darkened, Meinecke's political perception grew more piercing, and, more important still, his keen mind began to attract the more thoughtful of the German statesmen. Richard von Kühlmann, secretary of state in the Foreign Office, discussed with him the problems of international politics, and Theobald von Bethmann Hollweg, Germany's hapless chancellor, consulted him on domestic issues. Meinecke realized that the intricacies of power politics went far beyond the naïve assumptions of the academician. He abandoned his imperialistic projects and began to work for a peace by compromise without territorial gains for any of the great powers, a peace á la Hubertusburg.[14]

However, he also came to understand that Germany's domestic structure was superannuated and that a more equitable representation of the working class was imperative. His voice was heard in many quarters, but his advice was rarely heeded. Beyond the concrete problems which presented themselves was Meinecke's emerging comprehension that the nation-state in which he had so strongly believed was no longer a sufficient answer to the political exigencies of the times. The specter of the Leviathan state had raised its ugly head and had shown what naked power could do. Hence, new questions began to crowd Meinecke's mind: What was power? What lay at the bottom of the conflict which seemed about to sever the occidental world through its very axis? And what was Germany's position in Europe; had her evolution been essentially different from that of the Western democracies? Many years were to pass before Meinecke would venture to offer his answer to these queries. The Marxist-Leninist interpretation of the great crisis appeared unacceptable to Meinecke; world revolution and the revolt of the masses were, in his eyes, the greatest danger to Western civilization.[15] On the other hand, by the time the war came to an end, he understood that the old aristocratic and monarchic Germany was doomed. The downfall of the empire filled him with grief but not with despair. He accepted the Weimar Republic as a necessity and was ready to work for democracy, not from any enthusiasm but from reasoned convictions. Like other intellectuals, such as Ernst Troeltsch and Walther Rathenau, he joined the ranks of the new Democratic party. Many of his students, however, remained the ardent nationalists they had been in 1914.

Meinecke's doubts about the nature and justification of power that World War I had germinated in his mind were crystallized in his book, *Die Idee der Staatsräson in der modern Geschichte*.[16] Originally he had planned to show in a single investigation how the doctrine of the *raison d'état* and modern historical consciousness had arisen from the same root, but he soon realized that he would have to carry out this enterprise in two separate works. He first tackled the problem of the *raison d'état*, or, more clearly, the doctrine of considering the interest of the state as the guiding norm for political action. Meinecke confessed that the extreme manifestations of power politics during World War I had opened his eyes to the dangers of politics divorced from any ethical code. The Versailles Treaty served to deepen the lesson; it led him into an historical investigation of the nature and function of power in human life, which begins with Machiavelli and stretches from Bodin and Rohan to Frederick the Great, Hegel, Ranke, and Treitschke. *Die Idee der Staatsräson in der modern Geschichte* is Meinecke's first book of European scope, and its philosophical undertones produced a varied response. There are those who consider it a history of Machiavellianism; others view it as an attempt to surmount the teachings of Machiavelli.[17] None of these interpretations hits the mark. Perhaps it should be judged as Machiavellianism approached through a guilty conscience. Meinecke could not subscribe to Burckhardt's and Lord Acton's thoroughgoing condemnation of power; neither could he any longer assent to the idolatry of power found in Hegel and Treitschke. The result is a dichotomy, a separation of ethics and power that defies reconciliation. The creed of the statesman, says Meinecke, must embody both the interest of the state and the fundamental moral principles of mankind. He stands, so to speak, between God and the devil, allowed to follow neither the voice of his conscience nor the urge to forget this voice. His was a dualistic position which could satisfy few, but which clearly entitles Meinecke to be called the historian of an age in crisis.

Those who have evaluated Meinecke's work seem to agree that the *Idee der Staatsräson* is his most important book and will outlast all the others. The theme appears to have been of passionate and personal concern. Although he was rarely involved in active politics, the mechanism of political power fascinated and repelled him at the same time.[18] The lines he wrote about Boccalini, the Italian writer, could very well be applied to Meinecke himself: "His passion for political judgment was devoted to a world which he detested, but which filled him with the greatest enthusiasm to understand. The very thing which repelled him morally attracted him intellectually." In general, it might be said that all of his major works were attempts to explain problems which worried him personally, problems which he felt he might clarify for himself as well as for the contemporary world.

The theory of the *raison d' état* was not only an important European theme; it had a special ring in Germany where the mystique of the state had been ardently embraced. Meinecke had come to recognize its dangers and its limitations. Yet, realist that he was, he could not altogether relinquish it. Thus this book ends on a note of doubt and bewilderment. Summing up his inquiries into the *raison d' état,* he says: ". . . since it entered modern consciousness at the beginning of modern history, it has always been puzzling, preemptory, and seductive. Contemplation can never become tired of gazing into its sphinx-like countenance, and yet never quite succeed in fathoming it. But it can only appeal to the executive statesman that he should always carry State and God together in his heart."

In the Germany of the 1920's, Meinecke's scrupulous attitude toward the dilemma of ethics versus power found small sympathy. Neo-Hegelians like Julius Binder and Neo-Machiavellians like Carl Schmitt rejected the idea of a dual obligation for the statesman and propounded instead the dangerous notion of the absolute imperative of political interest in the presence of which all individual ethics ceased to exist. The real significance of the book, however, lies in its contribution to the history of political ideas. Meinecke had discovered an older layer of European political thought indispensable for the understanding of the masters of statecraft such as Richelieu, Frederick the Great, Metternich, and Bismarck. Thus this work contributes to intellectual history on a broader scale and with deeper insights than Meinecke had previously displayed.

In this book there is a mood of philosophical reflection which soon led Meinecke into an even more complex enterprise: the genesis of historical thought itself. In Berlin he lived in close contact with Ernst Troeltsch, who considered the historical outlook in its most comprehensive sense as one of the characteristics of the twentieth century. In 1922 Troeltsch had published his *Der Historismus und Seine Probleme*. Together with Croce's earlier studies, it constitutes the first survey of the philosophical implications of historical consciousness.[19] After Troeltsch's untimely death in 1923, Meinecke decided to continue the labor. His was not the gargantuan intellect of his friend; he was a historian, and as a historian, he was more interested in the origins of historical thought than in its consequences for the future of Western civilization. The results of his investigations were published in 1936 under the title: *Die Entstehung des Historismus (The Origins of Historicism)*.[20] It is the third of his significant contributions to the history of ideas, a work completed when Meinecke was well past his seventieth year, but dating back to the very early reflections on the element of individuality, or uniqueness, in historical life.

German historians had long resented the positivistic attempts to bring human development within the scope of "scientific laws," which, they contended, violated two of the most precious elements of history: spontaneity and uniqueness. It was this outlook on human life that Meinecke tried to trace from the late seventeenth century to the present. He defines historicism in the following manner: "... the essence of historicism consists in replacing a general and abstract contemplation of human affairs by an individual one *(eine individualisierende Betrachtung)*." Meinecke did not hesitate to call this concentration on uniqueness the highest peak in the contemplation of things human. He described it as the final triumph over the older ways of thinking that were inspired either by religious norms, or by the idea of natural law, or by the idea of progress measured in quantitative terms.

The book begins with an analysis of Shaftesbury, Leibniz, and Vico; it moves into an evaluation of the historiography of the Enlightenment, with special emphasis on Voltaire, Montesquieu, Hume, and Gibbon. From English pre-romanticism, it moves on to Möser, Winckelmann, Herder, and Goethe, and ends with an epilog on Ranke. Critics have pointed out that this history of historicism ends at the very moment when historicism really came into its own, i.e., at the beginning of the nineteenth century, and that we witness its growth but not its flowering. Another problem stated in Meinecke's book, but by no means elucidated, is that of relativism, inherent in the doctrine of uniqueness.

The romantic concept of individuality led to the anarchic individualism of the nineteenth century and came to an end in Nietzsche's nihilism where all universal norms and values are dissolved.[21] Meinecke, on the other hand, combined an almost religious contemplation of uniqueness with a belief in an absolute moral law. But, as Carlo Antoni observes, it is impossible to reconcile the absoluteness and the universality of law with individuality when the latter is considered as a law in itself.[22] Thus, in the *Origins of Historicism* the idea of the individual remains much stronger than the idea of universal norm. All values become relative, a consequence which Meinecke was loath to admit. He held fast to the humanism of his youth, the humanism of Herder, Kant, Goethe, and Ranke. If it was a solution, it was totally wasted on his time, which by then had seen the advent of the revolution of nihilism.

Thus the *Origins of Historicism* reveal to us once more the deep-seated dualism of Meinecke's thinking, a dualism which was both his greatness and his limitation. As Richard Sterling said: "His personality joined a profound and tireless intellect with a finely strung conscience and poignant sensitivity to the problems of justice. In one sense, it may be said that the attributes of character ought to weigh more heavily than the qualities of intellect in any assessment of his personality."[23]

A great number of problems were explained in this history of historical thought, but an even greater number remained unsolved. Meinecke knew the limitations of his own genius; he did not dare to offer a solution like the one that Troeltsch envisaged: a new synthesis of the Western mind similar to the one Dante had undertaken at the end of the Middle Ages. But in fairness to Meinecke it should be stated that no one else has done so with any degree of success.

Meinecke might have tried to answer some of these questions more conclusively had it not been for the general conditions of his time. At the time this book was published, Hitler had triumphed in Germany. Meinecke had fought against the rise of National-Socialism both in the press and from his chair at the University of Berlin.[24] The rise of Hitler and his henchmen affected Meinecke in more than one way. Some of his close political associates were ousted or silenced; many of his students were forced to flee the country; Meinecke himself was obliged to relinquish the editorship of the *Historische Zeitschrift* in 1935. But perhaps more devasting was the ominous premonition of a second world war that began to oppress his mind. We possess today a volume of his correspondence which clearly reveals that he was one of the few German scholars who did not compromise with the powers to be, and who had the courage to state in his letters what he was no longer allowed to say in public.[25]

Meinecke spent the years of the Nazi rule in setting down his memoirs. They hold a certain charm, but do not rank with his contributions to intellectual history. In fact they contain passages which strike the reader as a return to the ideology of his earlier conservatism. The war did not spare him; he suffered privations —the hunger, the bombings—that a million others endured. The end of the war found him in Franconia living in a peasant house.

Once more his mind turned to the enigma of German history, especially to the question which has since puzzled so many observers: What could explain the advent of Hitler, and further, to what extent were the German people responsible for the greatest retrogression in European civilization since the days of the Black Death?

Meinecke's effort to answer these queries is given in a small book, *The German Catastrophe,* which appeared in 1946.[26] In spite of the flood of new source material since published, *The German Catastrophe* holds a ranking place among the documents of historical introspection.

Meinecke begins his analysis with a scrutiny of the two forces that merged in the Hitler movement, nationalism and socialism. He contends that they must be seen against the background of our entire occidental culture, against the conflict between the old hierarchic society and the revolt of the industrial masses. But Meinecke had reached the point where he could look with an impassive eye upon the forces which he had once praised, the Prussian state and the German bourgeoisie. The Prussian state, he wrote, had permeated the nation with its militaristic attitude; the bourgeoisie had closed its mind to democratic forms of government which alone could have brought about a reconciliation of the working class with the older layers of society. Thus the demoniac figure of Hitler is placed in the wider dimension of social history and social interests which tried to manipulate Hitler and his revolution only to become its victims.

The German Catastrophe was not a popular book in Germany, where the process of historical reflection became obscured by a repression of the past. Nevertheless, it ushered in a process of revisionism which is far from ended. From our point of view Meinecke, at this time well into his eighties, attempted a new approach in which intellectual and social history were combined. This new attitude is also apparent in other essays he wrote after

1945, especially his comparison of Ranke and Burckhardt *(Ranke und Burckhardt)* and his appraisal of the Revolution of 1848 in the essay so entitled which appeared in 1948. These essays reveal, if nothing else, an indomitable will to continue the task of the historian in a world which had changed beyond recognition from the well-grounded security into which Meinecke had been born.

When a large part of the student body revolted against the oppression of the communist-controlled University of Berlin, it found in Meinecke the leader to head an independent institution—the Free University of Berlin. To have become the key figure in so momentous an action is surely one of Meinecke's titles to lasting fame. The historical institute at the Free University bears his name. His life and his work show an amazing parallel to the life and work of Benedetto Croce, who also became a rallying point in postwar Italy for the forces of the free intellect. Meinecke's contribution to modern historical writing has proved surprisingly durable and has reached well beyond the confines of his native country. His work has been emulated, corrected, and improved in Austria, Italy, England, and America.

But at the end of this brief survey, we find ourselves still asking some of the questions that have puzzled us along the way. One of the problems that Meinecke never clarified is the relationship of the history of ideas to history in general. What is the place of the history of ideas in the general framework of the historical disciplines? Meinecke never tackled this problem. Croce, on the other hand, produced an answer which stemmed from his idealistic philosophy, an answer which may strike many as all too facile. Walther Hofer, who may be called Meinecke's last student, has promised us a theory of history derived from the basic ideas of the master.[27] In the meantime, every student of the history of ideas will confront the problem as best he can. Herder once wrote, "A history of opinions would really be the key to the history of deeds." This would seem to be a fair expression of Meinecke's creed. However, we have come to realize that the methodological problems of intellectual history are infinitely more complex. A synthesis of Meinecke and Max Weber may be the answer to our quest.

Dialogs Across the Centuries:
Weber, Marx, Hegel, Luther

by Benjamin Nelson

The contemporary imagination continues to be haunted by the fateful encounter between Max Weber and Karl Marx. How shall we assess their distinctive analyses of the roots of modern society? How estimate their prediction of the shape of things to come? What, if anything, do these immortal antagonists have to say to us about man's nature, condition, and fate? How much light does each throw on the likely predicaments of men and their cultures in the years ahead?

Before answering these questions, we might do well to state two of our central convictions, both relating to dialogs across the decades and centuries between men of the mold studied in this paper. Commitments of this scope represent basic decisions as to how studies in the history of ideas ought to be conducted.

First: Men of the stamp of Weber and Marx—as well as the others mentioned in our title—need to be recognized for what they were—men of extraordinary range, intellectual and spiritual titans, far removed from the general run of those who win mention in the annals of politics, science, scholarship, or learned pretense. Only confusion results if they are treated as mere disciplinary specialists, intellectual careerists, or salon publicists, prepared to trim their sails to each passing wind. Far from being academically detached or coldly calculating bystanders, both were intent on advancing man's self-knowledge, fulfillment, and freedom. Being, in their own eyes, makers of ideas at least as much as movers of men, they bent their utmost energies to establish the foundations of a scientific study of cultural change and are now counted pathfinders in the strategic fields of economic history and sociology. In today's parlance, they were "existentially oriented" thinkers and doers who held themselves responsible both to offer testimony and to witness with their persons in causes of "ultimate concern." Viewing themselves also as responsible mentors advancing along the highways marked by the great traditions of thought, they need to be understood in the light of the universes of meaning from which they drew their sustenance and to the progress of which they hoped to make lasting contributions.

Second: Inevitably, however, the answers which men, even of this stamp, offer to the alternatives they confront, appear couched in the idiom of their day. This is true not only of Weber and Marx, but also of Plato and Aristotle, St. Thomas and St. Bonaventura. Nonetheless, to historians of ideas who share the outlook here expressed, it is an established premise that lenses of many different ranges and powers, perspectives from many different vantage points, need to be employed in order to understand the structures of the intellectual universes of thinkers who deserve to be ranked as "planetary." However topical these men may seem at one or another time, it will be discovered that questions of ultimate significance are their abiding concern. The topical matter by which they are stimulated and to which they refer generally prove to be less the subject than the occasion of their profound efforts. Nor does any one of them feel free to carry forward his explorations without entering into a dialog across the decades and centuries with the principal mentors of the culture, the authors of the master perspectives which come down through the ages. For this reason, the answers they offer so regularly have the flavor of conclusive variants of a central hypothesis and, therefore, paradigm definitions of our fate.

And now to our questions.

Weber, Marx, Hegel

Do Marx or Weber in their major writings seem to be concerned to develop theories of human nature and social existence? Here once again appearances are deceiving. Their denials notwithstanding, both of them were obsessed by problems of a moral and philosophical-anthropological nature. Both indeed addressed themselves to the same themes with equal relentlessness; both engaged in sharp exchanges with the same philosopher-ancestor. In the case of Marx, this dialog with Hegel is the keynote of his life; in the case of Weber, the challenge of Hegel seems very remote. Weber, rather, seems to be preoccupied with countering certain exaggerations attributed to a young left Hegelian named Marx. We contend, however, that both men are understood clearly only if they are set against the background of Hegel's development from his *Phenomenology of Mind* to his *Philosophy of Right* and *Philosophy of History*.

Contemporary scholars ought not be too surprised by the suggestion that Hegelian motifs played so prominent a part in the encounter of Weber with Marx. Though Hegel has often been pronounced dead, his specter has led a charmed life in myriad corners of European intellectual life. Indeed, since the close of World War II, the shade of Hegel has been standing free in the center of the stage. Today, once again, variations on his central themes appear to many to constitute the central options of Western thought.

Marx offers endless dialectics illustrating the labor theory of value, the notion of surplus value, the law of "the changing organic composition of capital," the law of the falling rate of profit, and so on. He discourses at length about the Roman patrician and plebian, the medieval noble and serf, the modern bourgeois and proletariat. Once he has bid "Goodbye to Philosophy," however, in his *Theses on Feuerbach* (1845), he rarely deigns to speak about *man*. Where outside of his earliest writings does he discourse on *human nature*? Do not Marx and Engels already in *The Communist Manifesto*, even before the publications of their maturity, make plain that they have lost patience with people like Feuerbach, Stirner, and the "True Socialists," who all insist on referring to the essence of man, man's obligation to love his neighbor, man's need of justice, the ego and its own, and so on?

A similar aversion to speculations about man in the abstract seems to characterize the writings of Max Weber. In the crowning studies of his later years, we will find superb characterizations of the Confucian scholar, the Buddhist monk, the Hebrew prophet, the Puritan saint, and the modern bourgeois. One looks in vain in his pages for an explicit or coherent set of declarations suggesting a theory of human nature and a doctrine of man.

For Weber, history has the character of ceaseless flow, a river which runs down to an unknown sea. Life here below displays an unending "strife of values," among which it is impossible to decide by purely scientific canons and methods. Nowhere is there to be found a privileged perspective from which to judge and interpret this "struggle between the Gods," whose outcome was purposeless drift. Was it not for this reason that Weber eschewed the writing of narrative history in favor of a theoretical analysis of the form of development which unique constellations of historical events might or might not come to illustrate to great or lesser degree? His was the method of the so-called "ideal-type," that is, a method which deliberately took its point of departure from the observation that the working categories of historians and social scientists were not literal renderings of objective realities, but rather mental schemata which represented, in a highly artificial form, selected features of past history or structural possibilities which actual configurations might more or less institutionalize. Where, in a view of that sort, was there room for a doctrine of generic human nature?

Despite these reservations, I am convinced that true appreciation of the careers and works of both Marx and Weber will be denied us if we do not see that from first to last, both men were crucially concerned to ponder and explore man's nature, condition, and historical development. Above all, they were haunted by the fate and hope of man in evolving bourgeois technological society.

Marx seems to me to have been the starting point of Weber, as Hegel was the starting point of Marx. Indeed, the writings of both require continuous reference to the entire development of German idealism from Kant and Hegel to their own respective days. However they may oppose one another, both Weber and Marx are the heirs, executors, and gravediggers of the German idealist tradition. True, Weber appears to differ from Marx in many respects. It is well known that Weber had little use for the assumption that historical materialism, as taught by its dogmatic partisans, had been confirmed by empirical investigation. It is not so well known that Weber was ready to admit that the materialist interpretation might serve a useful purpose, as one hypothesis among others, in carrying on a comprehensive inquiry. He would not admit that it was a proven or, in any ultimate sense, a completely provable theory of history.

This well-known opposition in their models for explaining historical change is not nearly so important in the present context as the shadings in their images of man's nature and their assessments of the future of human civilization. For the sake of brevity, I would put the relationship between them as follows:

1. In certain basic regards, they shared a sovereign interest in the ways in which the mysterious tensions of fate and freedom in culture could be understood and applied in the fulfilment of man's deepest nature and historic vocation.

2. Both of them were convinced—Marx says so explicitly, Weber implicitly—that men are possessed of a generic human nature. After this, however, they part ways.

3. Marx conceives of generic man as a bundle of needs and potentialities—man is essentially a conscious, rational, creative, tool-making producer. Weber sees man as an organism given to spontaneous satisfactions of deep-seated impulses, but capable, too, of rational action, in the sense of action explicitly oriented to the fulfilment of self-imposed norms.

4. Both are, above all, philosophers-historians-social-scientific-analysts of the experiences and spiritual itineraries of men in the development of Western civilization, especially in the era of bourgeois capitalist society. But again they take different turns.

5. In Marx, the main clue to man's plight lies in the way in which the production of commodities thwarts the achievement of free human personalities. Marx believes that the understanding of the labyrinth which they are called on to destroy is to be achieved by historical recall of the expropriations, the self-estrangements and self-alienations, by which men were separated from access to the means of production, the means of subsistence, and their own true sense of self. The artifacts and institutions which now oppose men as alien powers begin as the products of man's hand and brain. Man makes himself and in the process undergoes alienation from himself, from nature, and his fellow man. The restoration of undividedness will come when Prometheus unbinds himself, when the expropriated proletariat overthrows the expropriating ruling classes.

6. For Weber, the distortions of man's culture represent a story of the march of the spirit of *rationalization*. This spirit which, in the West at least, had already left its ambiguous imprint on every aspect of man's culture, his behavioral norms, his social structure, his economic organization, his legal system, his scientific philosophy, has now established dominion over his own reason and spirit. Mechanism and technique were everywhere now barring the door to the feeble thrust of ideals and ideas, whether old or new. The tyranny of conscienceless Reason was expanding its imperious sway across the world. This was the true meaning of the always more rationalized universe which continued to be engendered by the spirit of "innerworldly asceticism."

7. Here in this last notion is the key, at one and the same time, to (a) the decisive contrast between Marx and Weber, (b) the largely unnoticed reversal worked on both Marx and Hegel by Weber.

(a) For Marx, true generic human nature is indestructible.

The nature men acquire in history may represent either a fulfilment or a perversion of the primary potentiality, but generic human nature, however it undergoes alienation and distortion, remains indestructible. The production of commodities is for Marx the beginning of a series of self-estrangements in which men become subjugated to the fetishes of their own invention. The categories of political economy, the theories of legal power, the contrast between the claims of the state and the dictates of conscience, are as much symbols of man's self-estrangement as are man's theologies of his self-immolation before the phantoms of his imagination. Nonetheless, in Marx's view, though men lose themselves in the labyrinth of their self-estranged phantasies, they are certain to find their way out. The way back is the same as the way forward, and both together comprise the way out. This is the re-instatement of true human nature, social nature, and a re-integration of each concrete, fully existing human being and the permanent establishment of a system of social relations in which man for the first time will be able to enjoy a genuine coherence in the pattern of his motivations. "Prometheus Bound" is only the prolog to "Prometheus Unbound."

(b) For Weber, there is no way out so long as the spirit of rationalization and its progeny—mechanical apparatus and mechanized organization—prevail. Indeed, a nightmare such as that promised by the law of entropy may now be upon us. Only a miracle of sorts will replenish the original springs of creative charisma, now running dry. Reason's "final transfiguration," to use Weber's words, may well have occurred. Indeed contemporary man seems to be doomed to a "life of mechanized petrifaction, embellished with a sort of convulsive self-importance." The spirit of functional rationalization has set up its citadel in man's psyche. The functionally rationalized spirit of the man of today is powerless to engender a new beginning. Not by forcing but by serving the spirit in utmost inwardness do we fulfill our spiritual estate.

Marx is Prometheus *Redivivus*. His thoughts are never far

from generic man, for whom he ardently proclaims the collective resurrection, the leap from the kingdom of necessity to the realm of freedom. It never occurs to him to ask how society, economics, politics, individual and group interests, will be arranged and administered in the post-historic period, the age following the leaps forward, which Marx preferred to think of as the beginning of truly human history.

What Marx looks to as the advent of a new era Weber regards as the death-knell of the hopes of freedom. What Marx greets as the ultimate in self-estrangement, heralding the final deliverance, is for Weber a fate from which no present relief is likely and no ultimate escape is possible.

One could, without excessively straining metaphors, put the matter in terms of theological symbolics: Being by temperament a Johannine thinker, where Hegel was often Plotinian and Paulinian, Marx sought to reveal that the "contradictions" might be—and needed to be—overcome here below by "practical activity" *(Praxis, praktische Thätigkeit)* rather than in the mind of God or the mind of the philosopher. Beginning with a critique of Hegel's *Philosophy of Right*, his effort was to promote the understanding and realization of the eschatological promise of Hegel's *Philosophy of History*.

Weber, a historian turned sociologist and philosopher of culture, begins with a critique of the Marxist critique of Hegel, and ends by correcting the eschatology of *Philosophy of History* by the wordly realism of the *Philosophy of Right* and the pessimistic dualism of two other of Hegel's mentors, Martin Luther and St. Paul. The prominence of these themes cannot be missed in the magisterial orations of Weber's last years—*Science as a Vocation* and *Politics as a Vocation*. But can they be detected in his writings in the decades of transition between the centuries— the nineties and the first decade of the twentieth century?

Let us turn now to the *Protestant Ethic and the Spirit of Capitalism*, which first appeared as periodical articles in 1904-05.

Weber's Protestant Ethic, Luther, and the Times of Twilight

Is it conceivable that Weber's *Protestant Ethic* was intended to serve functions other than the ones generally attributed to it? Did Weber have motives for writing this work which transcended his apparent desire to modify the Marxist account of the generation and influence of ideas? I am persuaded that the answer to these questions must be "yes."

In a certain sense the *Protestant Ethic* must be read as Weber's answer to the eschatological mystique of Hegel's *Philosophy of History* and Marx's and Engel's *Communist Manifesto*. Another occasion will have to be reserved for the full exploration of this statement. We will, however, anticipate the nub of the matter here by scanning the *Protestant Ethic* for Weber's unnoticed support of Luther and his ambiguous response to Hegel.

Weber's *Protestant Ethic* sets forth a sequence of themes which resound with growing insistence in each new instalment of his scientific and personal odyssey through the spiritual universes of the historic world religions. The themes, now sparely, now strongly scored, orchestrate Weber's inner struggle over the ultimate options confronted by all men and groups in the course of time: the option between world-affirmation and world-denial, or as Weber more characteristically phrased it for sociological reasons, the option between religious rejections and ascetic mastery of the world. Christ did not come to preach the affirmation or the social improvement of the everyday world.

From the very outset of his career Weber was skeptical about all efforts to reconstruct society in the light of the Christian commandment of love or the socialist injunction to fraternity. A new world free of blemish would not be made merely by confronting existing institutions with the Christian spirit.

Thus, at the Fifth Congress of the Evangelical Social Society in 1897, he pointedly expressed his opposition to the views of Pastor Friedrich Naumann, one of his devoted disciples. Naumann was wrong to pin his faith on the introduction of Christian principles into social action. Said Weber grimly:

> We are not striving for a world in which more men will have greater happiness. No one who sees the prospects of things anticipates that more happiness lies ahead in the forseeable future. We strive rather to promote the distribution of those traits of personal self-responsibility and striving for higher things which our culture has taught us to hold dear.

A radical dualist, Weber stressed the differences between the kerygma and the ways of the world. Whoever obscured this served men ill, consigning them to perdition, leading them to demonization. Though critical of the effects of rampant capitalism upon the established social and moral order, Weber would not identify himself with those who believed that the Christian way was the reorganization of the world in light of the Christian ideal.

Even as a youth in military service, he shied away from accepting the radical Christian social teachings of the influential American Unitarian, Edward Channing. No moral purpose was served, he believed, by assuming that Christ's pacifistic commandments were to be the imperative of conduct for man in this world. Indeed, he wrote, an absolutely unqualified emphasis on pacifism would have the effect of demoralizing rather than moralizing warfare. Against this background, the message of the *Protestant Ethic* takes on a new tone.

Every attempt in the modern era to remake the world according to God's plan had the end result of offering religious premia for worldly action and worldly ideals. "The Puritans wanted to work in a calling," he wrote, "we are forced to do so." And he meant, though few understood, that *we are forced to do so* precisely *because they* (the Puritans) *wanted to*. It was the strength of the Protestant desire to manifest God's glory in this world which generated the rational organization of conduct and produced the modern economic order. Today, Weber concluded, soulless and mechanized capitalism holds us enchained; we are born into a cage from which there is no escaping.

Was there any basis, Weber meant to ask, for expecting that a new appeal to remake the world in God's image would have any more desirable effect?

For when asceticism was carried out of monastic cells into everyday life, and began to dominate worldly morality, it did its part in building the tremendous cosmos of the modern economic order. This order is now bound to the technical and economic conditions of machine production which today determine the lives of all the individuals who are born into this mechanism, not only those directly concerned with economic acquisition, with irresistible force. Perhaps it will so determine them until the last ton of fossilized coal is burnt. In Baxter's view the care for external goods should only lie on the shoulders of the "saint like a light cloak, which can be thrown aside at any moment." But fate decreed that the cloak should become an iron cage.

Since asceticism undertook to remodel the world and to work out its ideals in the world, material goods have gained an increasing and finally an inexorable power over the lives of men as at no previous period in history. To-day the spirit of religious asceticism—whether finally, who knows?—has escaped from the cage. But victorious capitalism, since it rests on mechanical foundations, needs its support no longer. The rosy blush of its laughing heir, the Enlightenment, seems also to be irretrievable fading, and the idea of duty in one's calling prowls about in our lives like the ghost of dead religious beliefs. Where the fulfilment of the calling cannot directly be related to the highest spiritual and cultural values, or when on the other hand, it need not be felt simply as economic compulsion, the individual generally abandons the attempt to justify it at all. In the field of its highest development, in the United States, the pursuit of wealth, stripped of its religious and ethical meaning, tends to become associated with purely mundane passions, which often actually give it the character of sport.

No one knows who will live in this cage in the future, or whether at the end of this tremendous development entirely new prophets will arise, or there will be a great rebirth of old ideas and ideals, or, if neither, mechanized petrifaction, embellished with a sort of convulsive self-importance. For of the last stage of this cultural development, it might well be truly said: "Specialists without spirit, sensualists without heart; this nullity imagines that it has attained a level of civilization never before achieved."[1]

Weber thus proves to have been not quite the humanist liberal he is often said to be. The grim Lutheran inheritance remains deeply rooted in his sense of experience. For those who knew how to read between the lines, the *Protestant Ethic* was meant to serve as a warning to adherents of eschatologies of the inevitable progress of beneficent Reason and Utopia. Thanks to the triumph of the spirit of technical mastery so powerfully encouraged by the Calvinist ethic, Weber implied, the world was already over-rationalized and regimented. Would not world-renewers of every description—Marxian Socialists, Christian Socialists, and others—learn that programs of technical improvement inspired by inner-worldly asceticism were hardly the way to check the spreading of spiritual dross and unthinking mechanism. Could not Western man see that in this interim his main trust must lie in the mysterious advent and workings of charisma in the individual spirit and community?

At this point, the contrast between Marx and Weber takes on a strange aspect. Weber's manner of countering two of Marx's basic positions has the odd effect of showing up antithetical compounds in both of their systems. Weber challenged Marx's historical materialist thesis at its core: an idea or ideal could exert significant influence as a determinant of historical development. On the other hand, Weber challenged another thesis which Marx, were he alive today, would doubtlessly deny he had ever held, whatever the evidence might seem to say: the apocalyptic potential in the recovery of revolutionary ideas.

In this regard, the otherwise deterministic Marx was, in truth, visionary. Man's true social nature, Marx was convinced, would be resurrected in the searing process of bringing into being the rational, necessary, and therefore, regenerative ideal. In the same action, the vulgar "contradictions" of their social existence would be finally transcended for all times. It seems never to have occurred to Marx that even a reconstructed humanity might create a new engine of self-destruction.

Heroes of Apocalypse and Interim: Prometheus and Sisyphus

Weber's life and work come into the clearest focus when he is regarded as one of those self-appointed mentors of the "times of troubles" who seek to prepare their generations for the agonizing days ahead. Intent upon the defense of certain of the treasured values bequeathed by historic tradition, Weber enters into the fray against the heaven-stormers of every persuasion, who in their haste to establish Paradise on earth were ready to risk all, including tyranny and total terror. He stands forth as a post-rational moralist, or as we incline to say today, a post-Christian thinker of the "times of twilight." He is a demythologizing philosopher of the interim.

The nature and extent of Weber's break with the century of his birth are sharply rendered in the themes which sound ever more clearly as he nears the zenith of his life:

1. Western man must somehow learn at this eleventh hour to curb his apparently uncontrollable drive to rationalize all corners of the world. He must come to see that personal freedom loses ground as functional reason continues its relentless march in the world of human affairs.

2. Liberal religion and ascetic social Christianity to the contrary, Christ did not come to preach the affirmation of the social improvement of the everyday world.

3. All efforts to correct or reorganize the world by adopting the alleged norms of the Sermon on the Mount are attended by radical paradox. The Christian is charged in conscience to act out of unmotivated love in utter selflessness. But if that be the rule for each Christian in his spirit, it is also true that no man can escape being answerable for the wider implications of his acts. Every man—surely every statesman—is fated to experience

agonizing tension between the claims of the individual conscience *(Gesinnungsethik)* and the claims of social and political responsibility *(Verantwortungsethik)*. No good can come from confusing the Christian realm of spirit and the domain of profane existence. The everyday world of passions and interests cannot escape the blight of organization, force, and hierarchy, if public order and wider civil interest are to prevail. The appeal to prophecy with a view to abolishing "outer bondage" involves a maximum threat to the spiritual man's "inner freedom."

4. A grim Fate stalks the careers of ideas and ideals. Their pristine purity is sure to be diluted and even perverted. Bureaucratization was the fate of every imaginative impulse; standardization, the destiny of every new vision; uniformity, the outcome of every form-bursting work of spirit. This happened to Christ's *Sermon on the Mount,* to Luther's ninety-five theses, and was sure to happen to Marx's *Communist Manifesto*. Behind the prophet stands the bureaucrat. The spirit of innerworldly asceticism—above all, Calvin's summons to establish God's sovereign rule in every one of man's earthly relationships—had ushered in the triumph of mechanism, of technique, of routine, in a word the sovereignty of conscienceless reason. (How different all this was from the promise of Hegel's *Philosophy of History* and Marx's *Communist Manifesto*. Weber's mighty monographs on the social psychology and economic ethics of the world religions have these works as their almost invisible background.)

5. The age on which we are now embarked, Weber senses, is one of drift and hovering doom. In this hour of twilight before darkness, no one knows what the new day will bring, whether petrifaction or a new breath of spirit coming one knows not whence. The old gods are dead, powerless to be reborn. The churches remain open but there is no return to their abandoned altars. Nor can one pin one's faith in prophetic creeds fabricated by professorial visionaries.

6. In the interim in which we are all obliged to live, man's one way to express his spiritual estate is to cultivate his deepest

truths in utmost inwardness. While we wait, we must struggle to preserve our spiritual dignity by pouring our best selves into intimate communions. Not by force, but by serving the spirit do we tend the flickering lights of freedom.

There is no easy way to explain why these themes have not received their due among students of Weber. The oversight may be charged in part to the disciplinary and technical approach which has been generally taken to his work. Unfortunately, the central theological and philosophical context of his life and times have been largely overlooked.

In our previous section, we described the difference between Weber and Marx in the following way: Marx, we said, belongs to the company of French Enlightenment and the Hegel of the *Philosophy of History;* Weber, to the company of the Hegel of the *Philosophy of Right* and several of Hegel's mentors, especially Luther and St. Paul. The two titans have radically opposed sensibilities with regard to the times of interim before the last things. Weber's Paulinian accents present the sharpest contrast to Marx's Johannine vision.

In this regard, Weber reminds one of Luther's reluctant heirs, Burckhardt, Franz Overbeck, Kierkegaard, Nietzsche, and in our own time, Albert Schweitzer. He is a faithful helmsman remaining at his post though the landmarks are gone. His ultimate antagonists are the confident paragons of the everyday world, religious liberals after the fashion of Harnack, nationalist propagandists in the style of Treitschke, the café prophets of a return to the old religion, the industrial and political heralds of a gleaming future. The longer we meditate on Weber's life and work from this vantage point, the more we must come to see him as did his friend, Karl Jaspers, as a Sisyphean hero of an age of ultimate trials.

Regarded from the perspective of our own day, Weber stands forth as a thinker of cosmic proportions who undertakes to explore the calling of men in what some are now describing as the first post-Christian generation on the European continent, the generation after Nietzsche's proclamation of the death of God.

There is hardly a theme celebrated by modern existentialists from Kierkegaard and Sartre which is not sounded in a distinctive way by Weber. Where Weber remains unique is in the desperate (not despairing) effort to discover sense and promote sensibility and scientific understanding in the fact of the absurd. He is, above all, the philosopher-scientist-poet of the interim.

In one way or another, the ultimate claim of truth in the face of the universal "disenchantment," which had become "the fate of our times," is the message which animates every one of Weber's utterances from his early letters and lectures to his starkly pessimistic swan song, *Science as a Vocation:*

> The fate of our times is characterized by rationalization and intellectualization and, above all, by the "disenchantment of the world." Precisely the ultimate and most sublime values have retreated from public life either into the transcendental realm of mystic life or into the brotherliness of direct and personal human relations. It is not accidental that our greatest art is intimate and not monumental, nor is it accidental that today only within the smallest and intimate circles, in personal human situations, in *pianissimo,* that something is pulsating that corresponds to the prophetic pneuma, which in former times swept through the great communities like a firebrand, welding them together. . . .
> To the person who cannot bear the fate of the times like a man, one must say: may he rather return silently, without the usual publicity build-up of renegades, but simply and plainly. The arms of the old churches are opened widely and compassionately for him. After all, they do not make it hard for him. One way or another he has to bring his "intellectual sacrifice"—that is inevitable. If he can really do it, we shall not rebuke him. For such an intellectual sacrifice in favor of an unconditional religious devotion is ethically quite a different matter than the evasion of the plain duty of intellectual integrity, which sets in if one lacks the courage to clarify one's own ultimate standpoint and rather facilitates this duty by feeble relative judgments.[2]

His effort and accomplishment are not to be denied by pointing to one or another misstep he made in relating to the earth-shattering trails of his times.

To sum up: Marx is a prophet of the nineteenth century, a philosopher of apocalypse and transfiguration. For better or worse, he did not have to witness either the seeming triumph or the very real demise of his dreams of total transcendence.

Weber is a man of another stamp. He lives in the time of twilight turned deep night, the anxious hours before the menacing dawn of the calamity-plagued twentieth century. With mammoths and mastodons once again roaming the earth, Weber dares not pin his faith on the visionary reconstruction of mankind in a new order. Instead he struggles to preserve the image of man by stubbornly tending the flickering lights of freedom and truth in the pursuit of the ultimate calling.

In Weber's unforgettable words:

> Integrity, however, compels us to state that for the many who today tarry for new prophets and saviors, the situation is the same as resounds in the beautiful Edomite watchman's song of the period of exile that has been included among Isaiah's oracles:
>
> He calleth to me out of Seir, Watchman, what of the night? Watchman, what of the night? The watchman said, The morning cometh, and also the night: if ye will inquire, inquire ye: return, come.
>
> The people to whom this was said has inquired and tarried for more than two millennia and we are shaken when we realize its fate. From this we want to draw the lesson that nothing is gained by yearning and tarrying alone, and we shall act differently. We shall set to work and meet the "demands of the day," in human relations as well as in our vocation. This, however, is plain and simple, if each finds and obeys the demon who holds the fibers of his very life.[3]

What else is there for the faithful *non*-believers to do who can neither wait, nor not wait, for Godot?

The Declassicalization of Physics

by George Gamow

The Fall of Euclidian Geometry

The radical and revolutionary reevaluation of the basic notions in physics, which took place at the break of the twentieth century, has its roots in far earlier developments in pure mathematics. A black sheep among the postulates of Euclidian geometry was the statement that through any point in a plane one can draw *one and only one* straight line which does not intersect another given straight line. This postulate of parallel lines was conceptually more complicated than Euclid's other postulates, and it was suspected that it could be derived logically from these others. However, all attempts to turn the postulate of the parallel lines into a theorem met with no success.

During the early decades of the nineteenth century two talented mathematicians, N. I. Lobachvski (1793-1856) in Russia and J. Bolyai (1802-60) in Hungary, arrived independently at a very unconventional solution of the problem of parallel lines. If the postulate of parallel lines is independent of the others, then it should be possible to develop a logically consistent geometry different from the Euclidian in which this postulate is omitted. And, indeed, they were able to construct a geometry in which through any given point one can draw not only one but an infinite number of lines (lying within a certain angle) which do not intersect with the given line. The analogue of Bolyai-Lobachvski's non-Euclidian geometry is given by lines drawn on a saddle-shaped surface. (Fig. Ia) A decade or two later a German mathematician, G. F. B. Riemann (1826-66) developed another kind

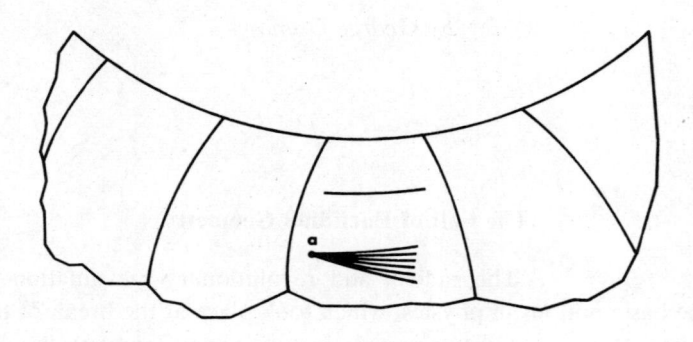

Fig. I-a

of geometry in which there are no parallel lines, and any two lines always intersect each other, as two great circles always do on a surface of the sphere. (Fig. Ib)

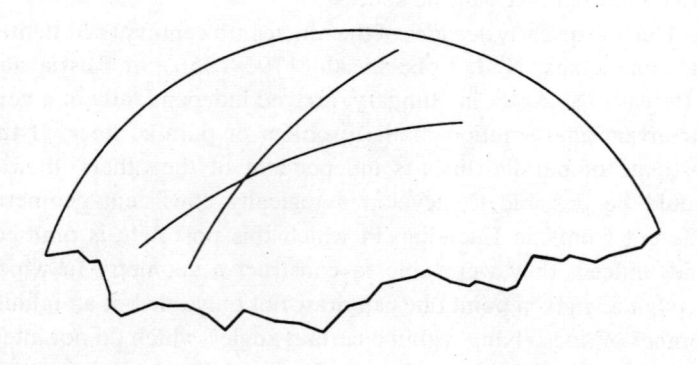

Fig. I-b

The work of Riemann resulted in the development of generalized geometry of the curved spaces with any kind of curvature and any number of dimensions. Although for a long time this geometry of the curved multidimensional spaces remained a pure mathematical abstraction, Albert Einstein found it very useful as a mathematical background for his ideas on the nature of gravity.

The Fall of World Ether and of Simultaneity

Prior to great events which took place at the turn of the present century, the science of physics was growing smoothly and undisturbedly. New discoveries and theories were added to earlier ones in a more or less continuous way, gradually increasing our understanding of the physical world, and it was believed that this process would terminate at some future time in the complete understanding of matter and energy. But there were some trouble spots, such as world ether—a hypothetical carrier of light waves —introduced late in the seventeenth century by a Dutch physicist, Christian Huygens. The discovery of the polarization of light proved that the oscillation of the light-carrying medium must be perpendicular to the direction of propagation. Such transversal waves can easily exist in solid materials which elastically resist any change of their shape. But the same waves cannot propagate through liquid or gaseous media which show no resistance to shape changes. The fact that the lightwaves are transversal leads to the conclusion that light ether must be solid material. On the other hand, since we see the moon, the sun, and the stars, it would follow that all interplanetary and interstellar space must be uniformly filled with it. How then can planets and stars move through space without encountering any resistance, and why is not the world ether crushed and ground by celestial bodies moving through it?! It was suggested that world ether has the property of plasticity (like sealing wax), behaving as a solid in response to fast-oscillating lightwaves, but as a frictionless fluid in respect to much slower-moving planets and stars. This suggestion never led anywhere and was contradictory to other physical phenomena.

For example, if lightwaves were the fast periodic deformations of the "plastic" world ether, the electro-magnetic lines of force surrounding ordinary magnets or electrically charged conductors would correspond to static deformations in the world ether surrounding them. If so, the static magnetic and electric fields in ordinary laboratory experiments would disappear in a negligibly small fraction of a second!

In the year 1887 an American physicist, Albert Michelson, undertook a very daring and ambitious experiment. He wanted, without any help from astronomy, to measure the velocity of the earth in its motion around the sun. His plan was very simple. If the earth moves through space with the velocity of $30 \frac{km}{sec}$, as astronomers tell us, we must observe an ether wind blowing on the surface of the globe in the opposite direction and with the same velocity. Thus, if we send a beam of light in the direction of the earth's orbital motion, lightwaves will be delayed or advanced depending on whether they move against or with the ether wind. Carrying out this experiment in a somewhat more complicated way, which is not pertinent to this discussion, Michelson found no delay or advance in the arrival of light, no matter in which direction it was propagating.

This experiment shook the entire scientific world, rudely contradicting the well-established beliefs of classical physics. After eighteen years of confusion there appeared in 1905 a short paper by a certain Albert Einstein, carrying an inconspicuous title: *On the Electrodynamics of Moving Bodies*. In just a few pages Einstein threw out the window the battered notion of world ether, and completely changed the ideas about space and time which had existed ever since these words were first used. The best formulation of what is space and what is time, to which even a Neanderthal man would subscribe, is given by Isaac Newton in his *Principia*. Writes Newton:

> Absolute space, in its own nature, without relation to anything external, remains always similar and immovable.

Absolute, true, and mathematical time, in itself, and from its own nature, flows equably without relation to anything external.

Einstein's basic idea was that instead of trying to reconcile the old and meritorious notions and definitions with the irreconcilable modern experiments one should rather change the old notions. If Michelson's experiment shows that the velocity of light (in vacuum) is always the same no matter how and where we measure it, that statement must be declared as one of the laws of nature and other things must be changed so as to abide by it.

Three centuries before Einstein, Galileo formulated in his *Discorso* a principle which is now known as the Galilean principle of relativity. He wrote:

> For a final proof of the nullity of all the experiments before alleged, I conceive it now a convenient time and place to demonstrate a way how to make an exact trial of them all. Shut yourself up with some friend in the largest room below decks of some large ship and there procure gnats, flies, and such other small winged creatures. Also get a great tub full of water and within it put certain fishes; let also a certain bottle be hung up, which drop by drop lets forth its water into another narrow-necked bottle placed underneath. Then, the ship lying still, observe how those small winged animals fly with like velocity towards all parts of the room; how the fishes swim indifferently towards all sides; and how the distilling drops all fall into the bottle placed underneath. And casting anything towards your friend, you need not throw it with more force one way than another, provided the distances be equal; and jumping broad, you will reach as far one way as another. Having observed all these particulars, though no man doubts that, so long as the vessel stands still, they ought to take place in this manner, make the ship move with what velocity you please, so long as the motion is uniform and not fluctuating this way and that. You shall not be able to discern the least alteration in all the forenamed effects, nor can you gather by any of them whether the ship moves or stands still. Of this correspondence of effects the cause is that the ship's motion

is common to all the things contained in it and to the air also; I mean if those things be shut up in the room; but in case those things were above deck in the open air, and not obliged to follow the course of the ship, differences more or less notable would be observed in some of the forenamed effects, and there is no doubt but that smoke would stay behind as much as the air itself; the flies also and the gnats, being hindered by the air, would not be able to follow the motion of the ship, if they were separated at any distance from it; but keeping near thereto, because the ship itself, as being an anfractuous structure, carries along with it part of its nearest air, they would follow the ship without any pains or difficulty. For the like reason we see sometimes, in riding post, that the troublesome horseflies do follow the horses flying sometimes to one, sometimes to another, part of the body. But in the falling drops the difference would be very small and in the jumps and projections of grave bodies altogether imperceptible.

Galileo wrote exclusively about mechanical phenomena, and, although he made one unsuccessful attempt to measure the velocity of light by observing the flash of a lantern carried by his assistants to one of the hills near Pisa, he had no modern equipment with which he could test whether a flash of light in the inner cabin of a sailing ship will behave in the same way as gnats, flies, fish, water drops, thrown objects, or jumping men. Michelson made that experiment and proved that light behaves in the same way as the aforenamed material objects.

From Newton's basic concepts of space, time, and motion (i. e., the change of position of objects in space in the course of time) it follows that the velocities must be additive. If a passenger runs with the velocity of 3 miles per hour through the cars of a train moving at 50 miles per hour, his velocity in respect to the ground will be 53 or 47 miles per hour, depending on whether he runs to the front or the rear of the train. According to the results obtained by Michelson, this additivity of velocities does not hold if instead of a passenger in a moving train we have a lightwave on the moving earth. Here the motion of the earth does not add or subtract anything from the velocity of light. Thus, in order to abide by the experimental facts, we have to discard the additivity of the velocities and substitute it by some other rule which fits the observations. According to the old Galileo-Newtonian mechanics, the velocity resulting from superposition of two velocities V_1 and V_2 is $V_1 + V_2$ or $V_1 - V_2$, depending on whether they are directed in the same or in the opposite way. Einstein's formulas for that case are:

$$\frac{V_1 + V_2}{1 + \frac{V_1 V_2}{c^2}} \text{ and } \frac{V_1 - V_2}{1 - \frac{V_1 V_2}{c^2}}$$

where c is the invariant velocity of light in vacuum.

In fact, if we combine the velocity of light c with orbital velocity V of the earth, we obtain:

$$\frac{c + V}{1 + \frac{cV}{c^2}} = \frac{c + V}{1 + \frac{V}{c}} = \frac{c + V}{\frac{1}{c}(c + V)} = c$$

and

$$\frac{(c - V)}{1 - \frac{cV}{c^2}} = \frac{c - V}{1 - \frac{V}{c}} = \frac{c - V}{\frac{1}{c}(c - V)} = c$$

Thus the velocity of light in both directions remains the same no matter how fast and in which direction the observation platform is moving. If we add the velocity of light to the velocity of light, we obtain, instead of $2c$:

$$\frac{c + c}{1 + \frac{c \cdot c}{c^2}} = \frac{2c}{1 + 1} = c$$

Let us try now a case of two "sub-light" velocities. Suppose that a train moves with the velocity ¾ c and the passenger runs forward through the cars with the velocity ¾ c. Both cases are physically possible even though the figures are well above the records of railroad engineering and the track records. Classically we would find that the velocity of the passenger in respect to the ground will be ¾ c + ¾ c = 1.5 c. "Nope," said Einstein, "it will be:

$$\frac{\frac{3}{4}c + \frac{3}{4}c}{1 + \left(\frac{3}{4}\right)^2} = \frac{\frac{6}{4}c}{1 + \frac{9}{16}} = 0.965\,c$$

i. e., smaller than the speed of light. Thus the velocity of light became the universal upper speed limit for all the velocities permissible in the universe."

The additivity of velocities in classical physics is a direct mathematical consequence of the Newtonian definition of space and time. Thus the only way to straighten out the matter was to change these definitions and to make space and time not so completely independent as Newton and all the physicists before and after him (prior to 1905) believed them to be. In fact, making these definitions, Newton just followed so-called "common sense" and they would not have been disputed either by the Archbishop of Canterbury, London dock workers, Jean Jacques Rousseau, Russian peasants, Immanuel Kant, natives of the Philippines, and other "common" men. But common sense is not necessarily the absolute truth, and, being backed by the results of Michelson's experiments, Einstein stated boldly that, in this particular case, common sense is nonsensical.

Let us consider a lightwave emitted at zero-time from the origin of the coordinate system, arriving at time t at some point P with the coordinates x, y, z (Fig. IIa). Since the light always propagates with the velocity c we can write, using the Pythagorean theorem:

$$x^2 + y^2 + z^2 = (ct)^2$$

Now consider another coordinate system x', y', z' which is rotated by some angles relative to the first one, and also moves in respect to it with a certain constant velocity v. When the lightwave is emitted from O, the origin of the coordinates of the primed system (O') coincides with O, and the clock in the primed system

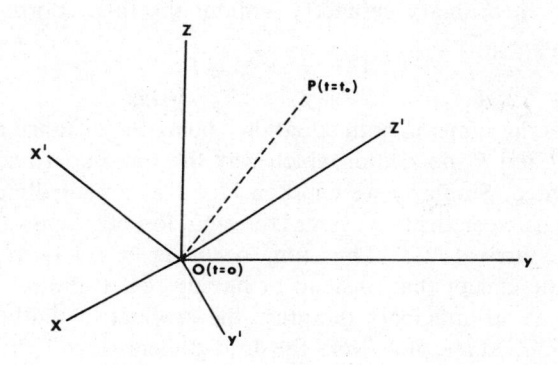

Fig. II-a. Geometry of 3-dimensional Euclidian space showing the motion from point 0 (x=0, y=0, z=0) at t=0 to point P' at t=t0.

reads: $t' = O$. Since the velocity of light as observed in the primed system is the same (c) as in the original one, we must write:
$$x'^2 + y'^2 + z'^2 = (ct')^2$$
Bringing the time term to the left sides of the above equation, we obtain:
$$x^2 + y^2 + z^2 - (ct)^2 = 0$$
$$x'^2 + y'^2 + z'^2 - (ct')^2 = 0$$
Both above expressions look like Pythagorean theorems in four-dimensional space, with ct serving as the fourth coordinate, except there is a minus sign in the fourth term. This can, however be remedied mathematically by using for the fourth coordinate ict where $i = \sqrt{-1}$. If we call that quantity (i.e. ict) τ, our equations become:
$$x^2 + y^2 + z^2 + \tau^2 = 0$$
$$x'^2 + y'^2 + z'^2 + \tau'^2 = 0$$
which is the conventional Pythagorean expression. It is easy to prove that the above equations remain correct if, instead of zero on their right side, we put any constant, say s, i. e., that
$$x^2 + y^2 + z^2 + \tau^2 = s^2$$
$$x'^2 + y'^2 + z'^2 + \tau'^2 = s^2$$

The fact that in the second equation we have s and not s' is not a misprint. In ordinary geometry without the time coordinate we also have:
$$x^2 + y^2 + z^2 = l^2$$
$$x'^2 + y'^2 + z'^2 = l^2$$
where l is the same, in both equations, being the distance between points O and P, no matter which way the three coordinate axes are oriented. Similarly we can consider s as a four-dimensional distance between the two events: the emission of a lightwave from O and its arrival at P. Thus time becomes in a way the fourth coordinate except that, instead of having real value as do x, y, and z, it is an imaginary quantity, the product of mathematical abstraction. Since, however, the four-dimensional Pythagorean theorem looks formally exactly the same as its three-dimensional predecessor, we can use it just as it is used in good old Euclidian geometry. (Fig. IIb) Wrote the Polish mathematician, H. Min-

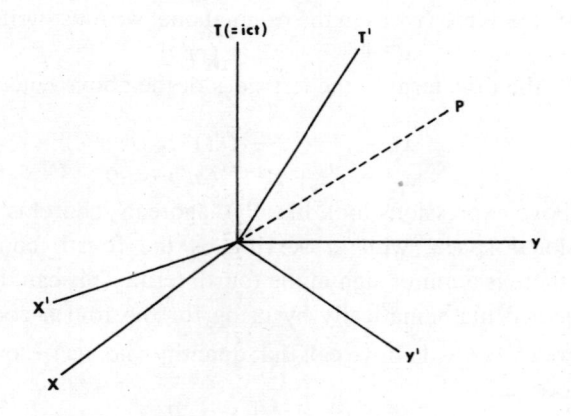

Fig. II-b. Geometry of Minkowski's world with 2 space—and 1 time-coordinate showing the same motion.

kowski, inspired by Einstein's first paper on relativity: "From now on space and time lose their mutual independence, and must be considered as two components of the four-dimensional continuum." But please do not forget that the fourth coordinate contains an imaginary factor $i = \sqrt{-1}$, which makes it impossible to turn a yardstick into a watch or vice versa.

However, according to Minkowski's four-dimensional interpretation of Einstein's theory, a *partial* transformation of a duration in time into a distance in space is possible if these intervals and distances are observed from two coordinate systems moving in respect to each other. One can prove that, looking on an object moving relative to us with velocity V one finds the length of that object (in the direction of its motion) reduced by a factor $\sqrt{1 - \frac{V^2}{c^2}}$ while the time intervals as shown by a watch attached to it are lengthened by the same factor. The yardsticks shrink and the watches slow down, but the sum of the square of space distance and the square of the (imaginary) time interval for two given events—which occur at two different places at two different times—remains invariantly the same. Another way of saying it is that if two events (i.e., something which happened at a given place at a given time) have space separation $\sqrt{\Delta x^2 + \Delta y^2 + \Delta z^2}$ and time separation Δt in one system of coordinates and the space separation $\sqrt{\Delta x'^2 + \Delta y'^2 + \Delta z'^2}$ and the time separation $\Delta t'$ in another, only the sum of squares of these quantities (using ict instead of t) will remain invariant and can thus be ascribed a definite physical meaning.

From the above-written equations it follows that if Δt between two events observed in one system is zero, it will not be zero in another system moving in respect to it. In other words, two events which are simultaneous in one system are not simultaneous in the other. Thus, time does not "flow equably without relation to anything external," as Newton wrote, but, quite to the contrary, depends on the relative velocity of one of the observation systems in respect to the other. In addition to the change in the distance- and time-scales, Einstein's theory also shows that the mass of the moving objects increases as its velocity approaches the velocity of light. The mass increases with the same factor $\sqrt{1 - \frac{V^2}{c^2}}$ as the distance decreases, and would become infinite if V could become equal to c. This prediction of Einstein's theory was confirmed shortly after its publication by direct experiments in which the mass of the fast-moving electrons (beta particles) emitted by radioactive elements was measured. Being unobservable at velocities which are very high from our human point of view (that of jet planes, etc.) but negligibly small as compared with the velocity of light, relativistic effects become quite appreciable when the velocity of light is closely approached. Thus, for example, the masses of elementary particles in the cosmic rays which move with the velocity of 0.999999 . . . . . . of the velocity of light may approach the mass of a ping-pong ball. But no moving object may exceed the velocity of light, since in that case its mass (i. e., the resistance to further acceleration) would become larger than infinity.

Free Fall and Gravity

Just as the roots of Einstein's special theory of relativity, described in the previous section, can be traced back to the writing of Galileo, Einstein's general theory of relativity, formulated by him in 1914, has its roots in Galileo's experiments on the laws of free fall of material bodies. Aristotelian philosophy, which dominated science in Galileo's time, maintained that some things go up (the flame in the fireplace) while other things go down (a dropped stone). Fire goes up because it is related to the sun and other celestial bodies; stones go down because they are related to the material of the earth. And the heavier the stone the faster it falls. Galileo doubted these conclusions of Aristotelian philosophy which were based on pure contemplation and not on any direct experiment. Thus, according to a story which may or may not be true, he climbed one day to the upper platform of the Leaning Tower of Pisa, carrying with him two balls, one of solid iron, another of wood. He dropped both balls simultaneously from the top, and the faculty members of the University of Pisa, who stood at a safe distance below, were astonished by the fact that, contrary to their beliefs, iron and wooden balls hit the ground at the same time.

Galileo's original experiment, which was more recently confirmed by using the most modern techniques, proved something important in the science of mechanics, namely that all material bodies fall with exactly the same acceleration. In mechanics one has two quite different definitions of mass: *inertial mass*, which characterizes the resistance of a material body to the change of its velocity under the action of an applied force—this mass is defined as the ratio of the force to the acceleration, i. e., the rate of change of velocity—and *gravitational mass*, characterizing the force acting on a material body placed in a field of gravity such as the one surrounding our globe. It is sometimes called "weight" which is a confusing and somewhat inaccurate definition since, transporting an object to the moon, we will find that both its inertial and gravitational mass remain the same, whereas its weight becomes smaller simply because the moon is less massive than the earth. The fact that on the surface of the earth all objects fall with the same acceleration proves that *the gravitational mass of any object is always proportional to its inertial mass*, a fact that does not follow from any other law of physics.

The proportionality of the inertial and gravitational masses remained a mystery for centuries, until in 1914 Einstein published a paper which connected Galileo's old finding with the deep-hidden properties of the forces of Newtonian gravity. In his special theory of relativity Einstein had proven that an observer locked inside of a windowless cabin, moving along a straight line with a constant velocity, cannot possibly notice that motion or measure that velocity, no matter which mechanical or electrodynamical methods he used. The above statement certainly does not apply to the case when the velocity changes. A passenger in a fast-moving automobile will be violently thrown forward if the driver steps sharply on the brakes or the car runs into a telephone pole. Thus, although there is no such thing as an absolute velocity through space, there certainly is an absolute acceleration.

In order to investigate the situation, Einstein started thinking what would happen inside of a closed cabin, floating in space far away from any star and uniformly accelerated by what we would call today jet motors. If the motors are not on, all objects within the cabin will have no tendency to move in any direction and will freely float in the air. After one puts motors on, the situation will change drastically, and all objects will be pressed to the floor as if pulled toward the rear of the cabin by gravity forces. Consider a man standing in the cabin, holding in his hands an iron and a wooden ball, just as Galileo did centuries ago. Because of the acceleration of the entire system, the feet of the man will be firmly pressed to the floor, and the two balls will press against the man's palms. But, as soon as he lets the balls go, they will continue to move side by side with the velocity with which the spaceship was moving at the moment of release. Being constantly accelerated, the spaceship will gain the velocity and in a very short time the floor of the cabin will overtake the two balls and they will remain tightly pressed to the floor. Oh!—will say the observer—there must be a gravitational field around here! And, if the acceleration communicated to the spaceship by the jet motors is equal to the acceleration of gravity on the surface of the earth, an observer locked in its inside will have no way of knowing whether his cabin rests on the earth's surface or speeds up in space far from any gravitating bodies.

If the equivalence between the field of gravity and the uniform acceleration is more than a coincidence, the same must be true in the case of electromagnetic and optical phenomena. Consider a light beam thrown by a flashlight attached horizontally to one of the walls of the cabin and producing a spot of light on the opposite wall. To follow the path of the lightbeam across the cabin one may install a number of fluorescent glass panes, as is shown in Fig. III. What happens if the spaceship is accelerated upward? During the time the light takes to travel from the flashlight to the first glass pane the spaceship moves up by a certain distance a, so that the fluorescent spot on it will be closer to the floor than the flashlight. According to the laws of accelerated motion first formulated by Galileo, the distances covered are proportional to the squares of time intervals. Since it takes light twice the time to arrive at the second glass pane it will hit *4a* lower. And for the third, fourth, etc. glass panes "the fall of light beam" will amount to *9a, 16a*, etc. Thus the beam, as seen by the observer in the cabin, will follow a parabolic trajectory very similar to that of a horizontally thrown stone.

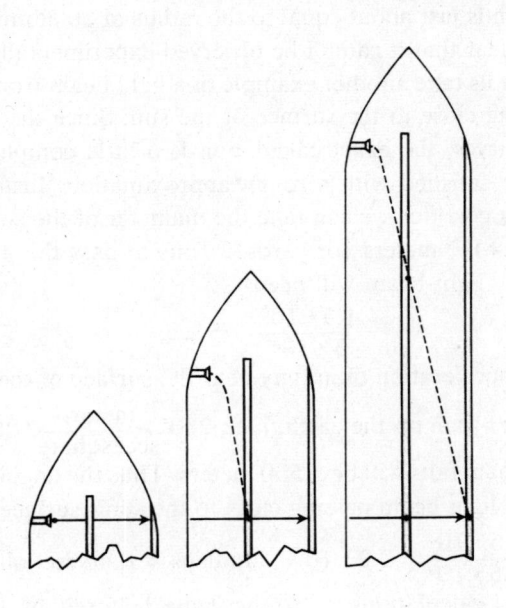

Fig. III. Trajectory of light beam in accelerated rocket.

If Einstein's principle of equivalence of gravity and acceleration is correct, we should be able to observe that bending of the light beam in direct experiment. Consider a corridor 30 meters* long with a light beam starting horizontally from one end of it. The time necessary to reach another end is the length divided by the velocity of light:

$$\frac{30 \text{ meters}}{3 \cdot 10^8 \text{ meters/sec}} = 10^{-7} \text{ sec}$$

* A meter is approximately equal to a yard.

According to Galileo's formula, the distance of fall during the time interval t is $\frac{1}{2} g t^2$ where g ($= 10 \frac{\text{meters}}{\text{sec. square}}$) is the acceleration of gravity on the earth's surface. Thus we get for the length of the drop of a light beam:

$5 \times (10^{-7})^2$ meters $= 5 \cdot 10^{-14}$ meters $= 5 \cdot 10^{-6}$ cm

This length is just about equal to the radius of an atomic nucleus, and it is clear that it cannot be observed experimentally.

But let us take another example of a light beam from a distant star passing close to the surface of the sun. Since the surface of the sun curves, the exact calculation is a little complicated, but we will be satisfied with a rough approximation. Instead of the length of a corridor we can take the diameter of the sun which is about $1.5 \cdot 10^9$ meters (or yards). Thus to pass the diameter of the sun the light beam will need

$$\frac{1.5 \cdot 10^9}{3 \cdot 10^8} = 5 \text{ sec.}$$

Since the acceleration of gravity near the surface of the sun is 28 times larger than on the earth, i. e., $280 \frac{\text{meters}}{\text{sec. square}}$, the distance the light beam falls will be 3,500 meters. Thus the angular defllection of the light beam passing close to the sun's surface would be

$$\frac{3.5 \cdot 10^3}{1.5 \cdot 10^9} = 2.3 \cdot 10 - {}^6 \text{ radians} = 0.46 \text{ sec. of arc}$$

More exact calculations led to the value 1.75 sec. of arc.

When, in the year 1919, a British astronomical expedition led by Sir Arthur Eddington (the Germans could not come because of the naval blockade) went to the Cameroons to observe a solar eclipse—during which the stars close to the sun became visible—they found the same deviation of star rays as Einstein had predicted. Thus the Principle of Equivalence joined the other basic principles of physics.

Now let us approach the problem from a somewhat different angle. Consider three observers placed on the earth, Venus, and Mars (or on three spaceships) at the time when they are spread more or less evenly around the sun (Fig. IV). The three observers

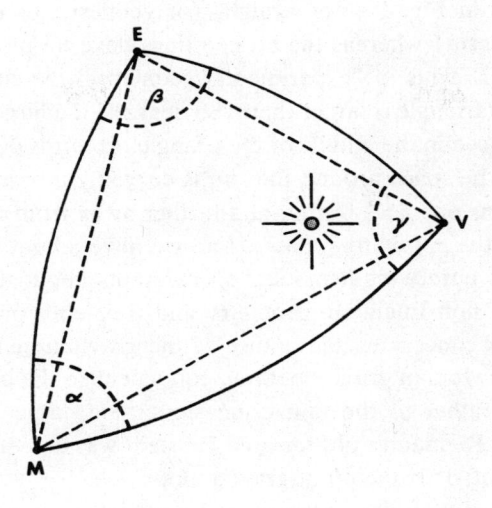

Fig. IV. Curvature of space around the sun due to the deflection of light in gravitational field.

carry precision teodolites and measure the angles: α, β and γ. According to good old Euclidian geometry the sum of these three angles must equal 180 degress. But here comes a complication. Since the light rays are bent toward the sun, the light beams will travel along curved lines (solid lines in the figure) rather than along the "really" straight lines (broken lines in the figure) and the sum of the three angles will become larger than 180°. The above statement is intentionally formulated illogically. For what is a straight line? When Euclid and the geometricians of olden times spoke about straight lines they considered this notion as self-evident. "What is a straight line?" "Well, don't you know, it is a line which is straight!" This kind of definition does not hold water in modern science. And if one speaks about straight lines in our universe one should give a direct method by which one can determine whether a given line is straight or not. And the most general and most logical definition of a straight line is: it is the path of a light ray in vacuum. According to that definition the solid lines in Fig. IV are straight (or geodesic, to use a more technical term) whereas the broken lines have no physical sense whatsoever. Thus in "experimental geometry" the sum of three angles of a triangle is larger than 180 degrees, if a large mass (the sun) is placed in the middle of the triangle. In terms of Riemann's geometry the space around the sun is curved, and this curvature decreases as one goes farther and farther away from the concentration of the gravitating mass. Here we have a contact between Riemann's purely mathematical speculations about the different systems of non-Euclidian geometry and Einstein's physical considerations concerning the nature of the gravitational field. The field of Newtonian gravity became equivalent to the curvature of space, or rather to the four-dimensional spacetime continuum. And using Riemann's old formula Einstein was able to develop a perfect relativistic theory of gravitation.

The Fall of Continuity and Causality

Toward the end of the nineteenth century difficulties began to accumulate in the problem of interaction of heat and light. It was well established by that time that heat is nothing other than the kinetic energy of innumerable molecules forming material bodies. It was just as well known that visible light is just a small section of a long spectrum of electromagnetic waves of different lengths bordered on one side by infrared radiation and macroscopic radio waves and on the other by ultraviolet radiation, X rays, gamma rays, etc. At that time two great British physicists, Lord Raleigh and Sir James Jeans, undertook the investigation of the laws which govern the transfer of energy between the thermal motion of the molecules in material bodies and the radiant energy in the electromagnetic waves.

The problem of the energy exchange between the molecules as a result of their mutual collisions was well under control, and the energy distribution between individual molecules was governed by the Law of Equipartition of Energy which was deeply rooted in classical physics. If we have a closed vessel containing, let us say, one billion molecules, the total amount of available heat must be shared equally among all molecules so that each of them will have, on the average, one-billionth of the total amount. But what happens if we try to distribute a given amount of energy among all possible electromagnetic vibrations which can take place inside of a closed container? Of course, we can put any amount of gas molecules into a closed container and then let them out one day, one year, or one century later. But we cannot shine light into a container, and let it out later by opening the window. The difference is, however, more practical than theoretical. Molecules bounce from the walls of the container (unless these walls are made from some porous material or react chemically with the gas) and will stay inside for an indefinite time. Light waves also are reflected from well-polished surfaces (mirrors) but in each reflection a fraction of light is absorbed by the walls and in practically no time light energy will be dissipated. Suppose, however, that we have an "ideal mirror" which reflects 100 per cent of the incident light. If we line the walls of the container with such ideal mirrors, light will remain inside indefinitely, just as gas will remain in a hermetically closed bottle. Ideal mirrors do not exist, but it is perfectly permissible to use this notion for theoretical consideration.

Another difference between a gas- and a light-containing vessel is that, while the molecules exchange their energy in numerous mutual collisions, light waves do not interact with one another and if the two beams of light cross in some point each will proceed as if the other was not there. (It must be noted, however, that the same is true for an ideal gas made of mathematical points, in which case the probability of a collision will also be infinitely small.) In order to permit energy exchange between different wavelengths of light we may introduce (theoretically, of course) a tiny particle of coal dust which, being black, is able to absorb and emit all wavelengths. Being very small, this coal-dust particle will not distort the thermal balance of the system but will permit energy exchange, however, between all modes of vibrations existing in the box.

What will be the result of such an energy exchange? The equipartition theorem tells us that all available radiant energy will be equally distributed among all possible modes of vibration. But how many modes of vibration have we here? The longest wave will apparently have two nodes at the opposite walls of the container as is shown by curve *a* in Fig. V (for simplicity's sake

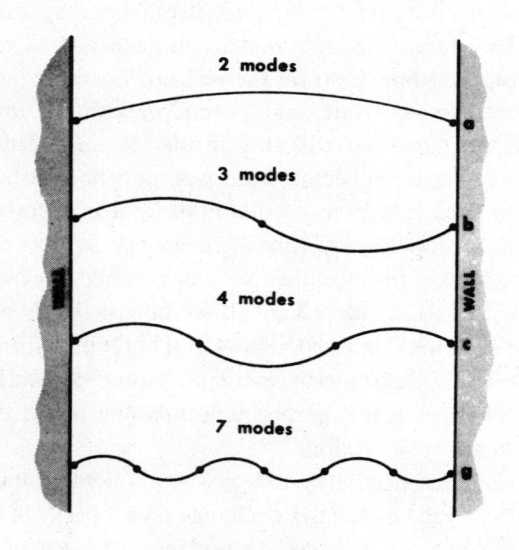

Fig. V. Different modes of vibrations in one dimensional case (as for violin strings).

we consider here only one propagation direction). The next wave (*b*) will have two nodes at the walls and one in the middle. The next one (*c*) will have two nodes inside the container, the next three nodes, etc., etc. Since there is no lower limit to the length of waves, we will have an infinity of possible modes of vibration and, whatever is the total amount of energy, the energy received by each mode will be zero. This so-called Jeans' paradox or ultraviolet catastrophe not only contradicts the observed facts but common sense itself. Indeed, lighting a few logs in the fireplace, we will first see the red light of burning wood, then the violet and ultraviolet lights, then the X ray and the deadly gamma rays. Clearly this cannot be true.

In the year 1900 a German physicist, Max Planck, made a revolutionary proposal to remedy the situation. He had shown that the ultraviolet catastrophe can be avoided if one postulates that the energy of light rays (visible as well as invisible) does not vary continuously, as was always assumed in classical physics, but in jumps. Just as a three-way electric bulb can have only three different brightnesses, depending on how one turns the switch, an atom can emit light only in definite portions which have received a name of light quanta or photons. The energy of a light quantum depends on its frequency (i. e., the number of vibrations per second) and is defined by the simple expression

$$E = h\nu$$

where ν is the frequency and h a universal constant known as quantum constant or Planck's constant. Its numerical value as expressed in conventional units is extremely small, being 0.0000000000000000000000000000677 in the metric system. Because of the low value of Planck's constant the amount of energy carried by a single light quantum is extremely small, and a weak source of light emits billions upon billions of light quanta every second. Thus for a human eye or a photographic camera, the fact that light consists of minute portions of energy is just as unimportant as the fact that the water we drink consists of individual molecules. But when one digs into the microcosm of atomic processes, the quantization of radiant energy becomes of paramount importance and prevents visible light from becoming ultraviolet rays, X rays, and gamma rays.

During the first two decades which followed Planck's epoch-making proposal, the theory of light quanta became firmly established in physics. Albert Einstein showed that the hypothesis of light quanta leads to a simple explanation of the so-called photoelectric effect, i. e., the emission of electrons from the metallic surfaces illuminated by ultraviolet light. Some years later Arthur Compton performed a famous experiment, studying the collisions between the X ray quanta and the loosely-bound atomic electrons. Everything fitted perfectly, and there was no doubt that radiant energy is not continuous but consists of well-defined energy packages, available as one, two, three or more packages, but never one-and-a-half, or two-and-three-quarters, etc.

Proceeding parallel to the progress in the field of radiant energy were the studies of atoms which, after all, are primarily responsible for the emission and absorption of radiation. In his famous experiments carried out in 1911, Lord Rutherford of Nelson (just Ernest Rutherford, Ph.D., at that time) showed that the atoms of different elements resemble somewhat our planetary system with a massive nucleus (playing the role of the sun) in the center and a swarm of electrons revolving around it along circular or elliptical orbits. This model of an atom, even though it was a direct consequence of well-planned and carefully executed experiments, ran immediately into a crushing contradiction with the basic facts known to classical physics. In contrast to planets of the solar system, electrons carry a very large negative electric charge. Thus, swirling around a positively-charged nucleus they were expected to emit intensive electromagnetic waves, rapidly dissipating their energy. It was easy to calculate on the basis of classical electrodynamics that each atomic electron would lose all its kinetic energy and fall into the nucleus within one hundred-millionth of a second. This conclusion did not agree with the known stability of the atomic system.

At the time Rutherford hit upon this model of an atom, the young Danish physicist Niels Bohr arrived in England to study with him the problems of the atom. Bohr realized at once that Rutherford's discoveries called for drastic changes in classical mechanics, which was hereto used to describe the motion of electrons within the atom. Being aware of Max Planck's theory of light quanta, Bohr asked himself why the mechanical energy of atomic electrons should not be quantized too. This would make an atom somewhat similar to an automobile transmission box which one could put into first, second, or third gear, but never into first-and-a-half, or second-and-three-quarters, etc. Of course, it would completely violate the classical laws of physics, but if a drastic contradiction arises the theory should be adjusted to experimental findings and not vice versa. The circular or elliptical motion of electrons in the electric field of nuclear charge is more complicated than the propagation of electromagnetic waves, but it only meant that more complicated rules had to be found for the quantization of mechanical systems.

Assuming first, for the sake of simplicity, that atomic electrons move along circular orbits, Bohr calculated that the electron in a hydrogen atom must move along the circle with the radii proportional to the squares of integer numbers. Thus the radii of the second, third, fourth, etc., quantum orbits must be respectively $4 (= 2^2)$, $9 (= 3^2)$, $16 (= 4^2)$, etc., times larger than the radius of the first orbit (see Fig. VI). In the normal state of a hydro-

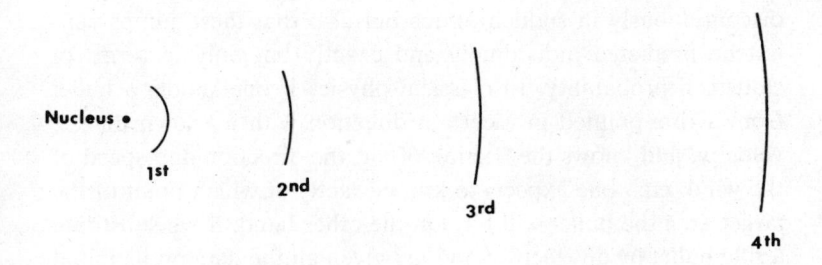

Fig. VI. Electron orbits in hydrogen atom.

gen atom (i. e., in the state of lowest energy) electrons move along the first quantum orbit. When the atom becomes excited, i. e., receives an excess energy due to a collision with a fast, free electron or a light quantum, the atomic electron is lifted to the second, third, or higher quantum orbit in the atom. Then in a course of about one hundred-millionth of a second the excited electron jumps back down to a lower energy orbit, emitting the excess energy in the form of a light quantum. Using this model, Bohr was able to explain in detail the observed spectrum of hydrogen, and in the course of a decade the quantum models of more complicated atoms were also understood. The introduction of light quanta and quantum orbits in the theory of interaction between atoms and radiation resulted in deep changes in our thinking about the atomic world. No more can one speak about the continuous motion of material particles and smooth changes of their energy. All phenomena in the atomic world take place in jumps and the energy liberated in one jump is used by another system making a jump in the opposite direction. Of course, because of the smallness of the quanta of energy one can disregard their existence in large-scale phenomena where billions upon billions of individual quanta are involved. But in the atomic world things look much different from the way they do in the familiar world of classical physics.

A very important difference between the classical and quantum physics is not only that the motion and energy changes take place discontinuously in sudden jumps but also that these jumps cannot be predicted individually and exactly but only in terms of statistical probability. In classical physics if one shoots a bullet from a rifle pointed in a certain direction with a known muzzle velocity, and knows the friction of air, the direction and speed of the wind, etc., one expects to know exactly at which point of the target area the bullet will hit. On the other hand, if we substitute a rifle bullet by an electron and are given all the data on its initial motion, all one can do is to predict the probability that this electron will hit the target at a given distance from the bull's eye. The difference between the two cases lies entirely in the difference between the masses of the two projectiles; a few ounces in the case of a bullet and 0.000000000000000000000000003 ounces in the case of an electron. The reason for this unpredictability of the exact motion of a given projectile lies in the quantization of energy with which it interacts with its surroundings. For a bullet the interaction with the air through which it flies amounts to billions upon billions of energy quanta and can easily be assumed to be continuous. For an electron it may be just a few energy quanta, and what will actually happen during its flight is subject to a law of chance.

This important difference between the large scale motion was first discovered by a German physicist, Werner Heisenberg, and is known as the *Principle of Uncertainty*. In the microworld we can no longer use the Newtonian notion of trajectory and have to introduce a new notion of *probability* wave, the intensity of which tells us about the chances to find a particle in one or another spot. The theory of probability wave, usually known as wave mechanics, was first introduced in 1924 by a French physicist, Louis de Broglie, and later developed by an Austrian physicist, Erwin Schrödinger. It accounts completely for all observed atomic phenomena in a probabilistic way, and its failure to make an *exact* prediction should not be blamed on the incompleteness of mathematical theory but rather on the properties of nature, which stubbornly refuses to be deterministic on the scale of atomic phenomena.

Notes

INTRODUCTION

1. Albert Einstein, Leopold Infield, *The Evolution of Physics* (New York: Simon & Schuster, 1961), 294.
2. Max Weber, *Gesammelte Aufsaetze zur Wissenschaftslehre* (Tübingen: Mohr, 1951), 191.
3. Weber, *Ibid.*, 208.

THE REORIENTATION OF AMERICAN CULTURE IN THE 1890'S

1. Allan Houston Macdonald, *Richard Hovey, Man & Craftsman* (Durham, N.C., 1957), 128-29. The present study has been assisted by a grant from the Faculty Research Fund of the Horace H. Rackham School of Graduate Studies of the University of Michigan.
2. Frederick Rudolph, *The American College and University: A History* (New York, 1962), 373-93; Ernest Earnest, *Academic Procession: An Informal History of the American College, 1636 to 1953* (Indianapolis, 1953), 220-29; Foster Rhea Dulles, *America Learns to Play* (Gloucester, Mass., 1959), 264; John Allen Krout, *Annals of American Sport* (New Haven, 1929), 225.
3. Theodore Roosevelt, *The Strenuous Life: Essays and Addresses* (New York, 1900), 8, 20-21.
4. *The Selected Writings of John Jay Chapman*, ed. Jacques Barzun (New York, 1957), 248-50; Henry James, *The Ambassadors* (New York, 1930), 149. On James's significance in this respect see Philip Rahv, *Image and Idea: Twenty Essays on Literary Themes* (Norfolk, Conn., 1957), 7-25.

NOTES—PP. 25 TO 32

5. *A Dictionary of Americanisms on Historical Principles*, ed. Mitford M. Mathews (Chicago, 1951). On "stuffed shirt" see also Thomas Beer, *Hanna, Crane, and The Mauve Decade* (New York, 1941), 97.

6. "Recording Time of Employees," *Scientific American*, LXIX (August 12, 1893), 101.

7. Frank Luther Mott, *A History of American Magazines, 1885-1905* (Cambridge, Mass., 1957), 369-70, 377-78; Frederick W. Cozens and Florence S. Stumpf, *Sports in American Life* (Chicago, 1953), 155; Harold Seymour, *Baseball: The Early Years* (New York, 1960), 345-58.

8. Dulles, *America Learns to Play*, 226-27; Krout, *Annals*, 227-31.

9. Mott, *American Magazines*, 316-17; Robert Lewis Taylor, "Physical Culture," *New Yorker*, XXVI (October 21, 1950), 47-50.

10. Lawrence A. Cremin, *The Transformation of the School: Progressivism in American Education, 1876-1957* (New York, 1961), 77; Margaret H. Underwood, *Bibliography of North American Minor Natural History Serials in the University of Michigan Libraries* (Ann Arbor, 1954). For general background see Hans Huth, *Nature and the American: Three Centuries of Changing Attitudes* (Berkeley, Cal., 1957), which reminds us that urban interest in the out-of-doors grew steadily during the preceding decades, though it increased most sharply after 1890.

11. Francis W. Halsey, "The Rise of the Nature Writers," *Review of Reviews*, XXVI (November, 1902), 567-71.

12. *Birds*, II (December, 1897), back cover; *Bird Lore*, I (1899), 28.

13. James D. Hart, *The Popular Book: A History of America's Literary Taste* (New York, 1950), 214-15; Grant C. Knight, *The Critical Period in American Literature* (Chapel Hill, 1951), 121.

14. Macdonald, *Hovey*, 141-50.

15. David Ewen, *Panorama of American Popular Music* (Englewood Cliffs, 1957), 100-05, 142; *One Hundred Years of Music in America*, ed. Paul Henry Lang (New York, 1961), 143-47; Gilbert Chase, *America's Music From the Pilgrims to the Present* (New York, 1955), 433-45. See also the detailed account by Rudi Blesh and Harriet Janis, *They All Played Ragtime: The True Story of an American Music* (New York, 1959).

16. Bernarr Macfadden, *The Power and Beauty of Superb Womanhood* (New York, 1901), 23; William Dean Howells, *Suburban Sketches* (Boston, 1872), 96; James Fullarton Muirhead, *The Land of Contrasts* (London, 1898), 127.

17. Quoted from *Munsey's Magazine*, 1896, in Mott, *American Magazines*, 370-71.

18. Eleanor Flexner, *Century of Struggle: The Woman's Rights Movement in the United States* (Cambridge, Mass., 1959), 222-25.

19. James C. Malin, *Confounded Rot about Napoleon: Reflections upon Science and Technology, Nationalism, World Depression of the Eighteen-Nineties, and Afterwards* (Lawrence, Kan., 1961), 90, 185-97.

20. Cozens and Stumpf, *Sports*, 112-14. On cheer leaders see Muirhead,

Land of Contrasts, 114; on jingoism, Richard Hofstadter, "Manifest Destiny and the Philippines," in *America in Crisis*, ed. Daniel Aaron (New York, 1952), 173-200.

21. Isaac Goldberg, *Tin Pan Alley* (New York, 1930), 166; Krout, *Annals*, 227; Theodore Roosevelt, "Value of an Athletic Training," *Harper's Weekly*, XXXVII (December 23, 1893), 1236.

22. Halsey, "Rise of the Nature Writers," *Review of Reviews*, XXVI, 571; Gerhard Masur, *Prophets of Yesterday: Studies in European Culture, 1890-1914* (New York, 1961), 356-59. The appeal of Haggard and Kipling in America is indicated in Hart, *Popular Book*, 309-10.

23. Frances Elizabeth McFall ("Sarah Grand"), *The Heavenly Twins* (New York, 1893), 193; Frank Luther Mott, *Golden Multitudes: The Story of Best Sellers in the United States* (New York, 1947), 181-82.

24. Muirhead, *Land of Contrasts*, 106 ff.; *Sports & Athletics in 1908* (London, 1908), 13.

25. Paul de Rousiers, *American Life* (Paris, 1892), 324-33; Nat Fleischer, *The Heavyweight Championship* (New York, 1949), xiii.

26. Holbrook Jackson, *The Eighteen Nineties* (Harmondsworth, England, 1939), 28.

27. Harry Thurston Peck, "Migration of Popular Songs," *Bookman*, II (September, 1895), 101; Chase, *America's Music*, 438.

28. Maurice F. Brown, "Santayana's American Roots," *New England Quarterly*, XXXIII (June, 1960), 147-63; Eric McKitrick, "Edgar Saltus of the Obsolete," *American Quarterly*, III (Spring, 1951), 22-35; Max I. Baym, *The French Education of Henry Adams* (New York, 1951), 67.

29. Harold Frederic, *The Damnation of Theron Ware* (New York, 1896), 484.

30. Roger B. Salomon, *Twain and the Image of History* (New Haven, 1961), 199.

31. William Graham Sumner, *Social Darwinism: Selected Essays*, ed. Stow Persons (New York, 1963), 179-80; Rollo Ogden, *Life and Letters of Edwin Lawrence Godkin*, 2 vols. (New York, 1907), II, 186-87, 199, 202.

32. Brooks Adams, *The Law of Civilization and Decay* (New York, 1895); Henry Adams, *The Degradation of the Democratic Dogma* (New York, 1920).

33. Woodrow Wilson, *Congressional Government* (Boston, 1885), 5; Barrett Wendell, *A Literary History of America* (New York, 1900), 518.

34. Richard Burton, "Degenerates and Geniuses," *The Critic*, XXV (August 11, 1894), 85-86. For a general review of this intensely animated discussion see Milton Painter Foster, "The Reception of Max Nordau's *Degeneration* in England and America," University Microfilms, No. 1807 (Ann Arbor, 1954).

35. Quoted in George Mowry, *The Era of Theodore Roosevelt, 1900-1912* (New York, 1958), 88. See also Donald Pizer, "Romantic Individualism in Garland, Norris and Crane," *American Quarterly*, X (Winter,

1958), 463-75, and Kenneth S. Lynn, *The Dream of Success: A Study of the Modern American Imagination* (Boston, 1955).

36. Van Wyck Brooks, *The Confident Years, 1885-1915* (New York, 1952), 218.

37. Arthur Beringause, *Brooks Adams, A Biography* (New York, 1955), 167-71, 186.

38. William E. Leuchtenburg, "Progressivism and Imperialism: The Progressive Movement and American Foreign Policy, 1898-1916," *Mississippi Valley Historical Review*, XXXIX (December, 1952), 483-504; John Higham, *Strangers in the Land: Patterns of American Nativism 1860-1925* (New Brunswick, 1955), 106-18, 144-45.

39. My indebtedness in the following pages to Morton G. White's *Social Thought in America: The Revolt Against Formalism* (New York, 1949) and to Henry F. May's *The End of American Innocence: The First Years of Our Own Time, 1912-1917* (New York, 1959) should be readily apparent, although they deal with other people and with a later period. I think the 1890's were more critically important than either book suggests.

40. On Turner's intellectual development see Fulmer Mood, "The Development of Turner as a Historical Thinker," Colonial Society of Massachusetts *Transactions*, XXXIV (1939), 283-352, and Lee Benson, *Turner and Beard: American Historical Writing Reconsidered* (Glencoe, Ill., 1960), 21-34.

41. Ralph Barton Perry, *The Thought and Character of William James*, 2 vols. (Boston, 1935), II, 251, 312.

42. "The Reminiscences of Guy Stanton Ford" (Oral History Research Office, Columbia University, 1956), 77-85; Ray Allen Billington, "Why Some Historians Rarely Write History: A Case Study of Frederick Jackson Turner," *Mississippi Valley Historical Review*, L (June, 1963), 3-27.

43. Frank Lloyd Wright, *An Autobiography* (New York, 1943). On Wright's development and qualities as an architect I am especially indebted to Vincent Scully, Jr., *Frank Lloyd Wright* (New York, 1960).

44. Perry, *James*, II, 700.

45. See especially his *Rise of the New West, 1819-1829* (New York, 1906).

46. Edward Bok, *The Americanization of Edward Bok* (New York, 1922), 238-45, 251-58.

47. Wright, *Autobiography*, 71. Cf. James's remark: "Your last two letters have breathed a . . . *Lebenslust*, which . . . nothing but mother earth can give." Perry, *James*, I, 414.

48. Quoted in Scully, *Wright*, 18; Frederick Jackson Turner, *The Frontier in American History* (New York, 1920).

49. William James, *The Will to Believe* (New York, 1931), 39-62, and *The Varieties of Religious Experience* (Modern Library, n.d.). These books were first published in 1896 and 1902 respectively.

50. "Whitman and the Influence of Space on American Literature," Newberry Library *Bulletin*, V (December, 1961), 299-314.

51. James, *Varieties*, 84. In print, Turner quoted Whitman only once; he turned more readily to Kipling. *Frontier*, 262, 270, 336.

52. John Burroughs, *Whitman: A Study* (New York, 1896), 223. See also Burrough's own response to Whitman (p. 103): "He kindles in me the delight I have in space, freedom, power. . . ." On Whitman's reputation in the 1890's see Charles B. Willard, *Whitman's American Fame* (Providence, 1950), 28-29, 216.

53. Perry, *James*, II, 258; Wright, *Autobiography*, 126-28.

54. For the European cultural milieu I have depended heavily on: Masur, *Prophets of Yesterday*; H. Stuart Hughes, *Consciousness and Society: The Reorientation of European Social Thought, 1890-1930* (New York, 1958); Morse Peckham, *Beyond the Tragic Vision: The Quest for Identity in the Nineteenth Century* (New York, 1962); Roger Shattuck, *The Banquet Years: The Arts in France, 1885-1918* (Garden City, 1961); Carl E. Schorske, "Politics and the Psyche in *fin de siècle* Vienna: Schnitzler and Hofmannsthal," *American Historical Review*, LXVI (July, 1961), 930-46; Arthur Symons, *The Symbolist Movement in Literature* (London, 1899); and Eugen Weber's essay in the present volume.

55. Hamilton Wright Mabie, *Essays on Nature and Culture* (New York, 1896), 231-32, 235-36, 241.

THE CONCEPT OF NATURE

1. *The Poetical Works of Wordsworth*, ed. Thomas Hutchinson (London: Oxford University Press, 1928), 207.

2. Edmond et Jules de Goncourt, *Journal: Mémoires de la vie littéraire*, Tome premier 1851-1861 (Paris: Ernest Flammarion, n.d.), 105 f.

3. George Santayana, *Scepticism and Animal Faith* (New York: Charles Scribner's Sons, 1924), 237 f.

4. A nicer discrimination would, of course, distinguish between these two: the "creationist" and the "matrix" theories of nature. And in fact Herbert W. Schneider has done so. See his "The Unnatural" in Yervant H. Krikorian's *Naturalism and the Human Spirit* (New York: Columbia University Press, 1944), 121-32. But the kind of nuanced analysis and exhaustive categorizing which occurs in, for example, the appendix of Lovejoy and Boas' *A Documentary History of Primitivism and Related Ideas* (Baltimore: The Johns Hopkins Press, 1935) or in Harold S. Wilson's "Meanings of 'Nature' in Renaissance Literature" (*Journal of the History of Ideas*, October, 1941) is obviously no part of my intention in this paper.

5. See Albert William Levi, *Literature, Philosophy and the Imagination* (Bloomington: Indiana University Press, 1962), Chapter II, "From Kant to Cassirer" and Chapter III, "The Teleological Imagination."

6. This distinction, for example, constitutes almost the complete rationale of such a work as Whitehead's *Science and the Modern World* (New York: The Macmillan Co., 1925). Compare in this connection

Chapters III and IV ("The Century of Genius" and "The Eighteenth Century") with Chapter V ("The Romantic Reaction").

7. Frederick J. E. Woodbridge, *An Essay on Nature* (New York: Columbia University Press, 1940), 4 f.

8. M. Mirabaud (pseudonym of Baron d'Holbach, *Le Système de la nature, ou Des lois du monde physique et du monde moral* (London: 1775), I, 15, 24.

9. *Ibid.*, II, 435 f.

10. Irving Babbitt, *Rousseau and Romanticism* (Boston: Houghton Mifflin Co., 1919), Chapter VIII, "Romanticism and Nature."

11. *Goncourt Journal, Op. cit.*, 108.

12. "Sartre s'était indigné; il avait aussi balayé tous mes projets de promenade; il était allergique à la chlorophylle, le verdoiement de ces pâturages l'excédait, il ne le tolérait qu'a condition de l'oublier." Simone de Beauvoir, *La Force de l'age* (Gallimard, 1960), 17.

13. This episode is to be found in Jean-Paul Sartre, *La Nausée* (Libraire Gallimard, 1938), 161-71.

14. There are, of course, some themes treated by Jaspers and Heidegger which reflect an older metaphysical interest which imply (although they never explicitly spell out) some concern with nature. For example there is Heidegger's treatment of *Die Weltlichkeit der Welt* and *Das In-der-Welt-Sein* in his *Sein und Zeit* (Tübingen: Max Niemeyer Verlag, 1957), 63-130, and Jasper's remarks on *Weltorientierung* in Vol. I and on *Transzendenz* in Vol. III of his *Philosophie* (Berlin: Springer-Verlag, 1956).

15. Rudolph Carnap, *Der logische Aufbau der Welt* (Berlin: Im Weltkreis-Verlag, 1928), 286.

16. For a brief treatment of the roots and the development of contemporary positivism, see my *Philosophy and the Modern World* (Bloomington: Indiana University Press, 1959), 331-46.

17. A. N. Whitehead, *The Concept of Nature* (Cambridge University Press, 1955), 2 f.

18. A. N. Whitehead, *Nature and Life* (Chicago: The University of Chicago Press, 1934), 9.

19. *Ibid.*, 25.

20. See Mary A. Wyman, "Whitehead's Philosophy of Science in the Light of Wordsworth's Poetry," *Philosophy of Science*, Vol. 23, No. 4 (October, 1956).

21. A. N. Whitehead, *Essays in Science and Philosophy* (New York: Philosophical Library, 1948), 35.

22. A. N. Whitehead, *Science and the Modern World* (New York: The Macmillan Co., 1925), 116 f.

23. Friedrich Nietzsche, *Werke in drei Bänden* (München: Carl Hanser Verlag), I, 1219.

24. *Ibid.*, 1221. "Wie anders und wie viel näher an den Menschen gerücht musste ihnen die Natur erscheinen, weil in ihrem Auge die

Farben des Menschen auch in der Natur überwogen, und diese gleichsam in dem Farbenäther der Menschheit schwamm!"
25. *Ibid.*, II, 127.
26. Ernst Mach, *The Science of Mechanics* (Open Court, 1942), Chapter IV, "The Formal Development of Mechanics."
27. *Ibid.*, 560.
28. Ernst Mach, *Die Analyse der Empfindungen* (Jena: Fischer Verlag, 1922), 9, 10.
29. *Ibid.*, 28. "Der Spuk verschwindet jedoch sofort, wenn man die Sache sozusagen im mathematischen Sinn auffasst, und sich klar macht, dass nur die Ermittlung von Funktionalbeziehungen für uns Wert hat, dass es lediglich die Abhängigkeiten der Erlebnisse voneinander sind, die wir zu kennen wünschen."
30. F. H. Bradley, *Appearance and Reality* (Oxford, At the Clarendon Press, 1951), 231.
31. *Ibid.*, 245.
32. *Ibid.*, 247.

THE SECRET WORLD OF JEAN BAROIS

1. Romain Rolland, *Mémoires et fragments du journal* (Paris, 1956), 21.
2. J. E. C. Bodley, *Cardinal Manning and Other Essays* (London, 1912), 89; Léon Daudet, *Le Stupide 19e siècle* (Paris, 1922), 99. In *Consciousness and Society* (New York, 1958), 112, Stuart Hughes suggests that the influence of William James "began its triumphant progress" after the turn of the century. Perhaps. But he had made his name in Europe some time before that.
3. Eugène-Melchior de Vogüé, *Lettres à Armand et Henri de Pontmartin, 1867-1909* (Paris, 1922), 139.
4. Jules Renard, *Journal* (Paris, 1935), 48; Maurice Barrès, "Examen," *Sous l'oeil des barbares* (Paris, 1922), 12, 14-15. One way of doing this would be indicated by André Suarès contemporary of Romain Rolland and Edouard Herriot at the Ecole Normale. Called up for military service, Suarès presented himself with a partition of *Parsifal* under one arm and a pint of cologne in the left hand. The antimilitarism of the Left has a great deal to do with the law of 1889 which, for the first time, forced a majority of educated young men to perform their military service. The anti-intellectualism of the military presumably stems largely from the same experience.
5. "L'Originalité du socialisme français," in *Tendances politiques de la vie française* (Paris, 1960), 53. The whole essay deserves study.
6. Adrien Dansette, *Le Boulangisme* (Paris, 1946), 364; Barrès, *Un Homme libre* (Paris, n.d.), 91; *Mes Cahiers*, (Paris, 1929), I, 37. Throughout the nineties, as unsuccessful candidate in elections at Neuilly-Boulogne

(1893, 1896) and at Nancy (1898), Barrès sported a mixture of nationalism and socialism. Significantly, he would only be elected in 1906 (the year of his election to the Academy), after he had abandoned this disquieting national socialism to become a *"républicain patriote libéral."*

7. Barrès, *L'Ennemi des lois* (Paris, 1892), 141, 176.

8. Vogüé, *Lettres*, December 30, 1893, 113-14; *Le Roman russe* (Paris, 1886), p. L. On the following page the author quotes Ségur's *Memoirs* on the mood of 1796: "Toute croyance était ébranlée, toute direction effacée ou devenue incertaine; et plus les âmes neuves étaient pensives et ardentes, plus elles erraient et se fatiguaient sans soutien, dans ce vague infini, désert san limites, où rien ne contenait leurs écarts, où beaucoup s'affaisaient enfin, et retombant désenchantées sur elles-mêmes, n'apercevaient de certain, au travers de la poussière de tant de débris, que la mort pour borne! . . . Je ne vis plus qu'elle en tout et partout. . . . Ainsi mon âme s'usait, prête à emporter tout le reste; je languissais. . . ." As he might well have done today, Vogüé adds: "Does contemporary pessimism express itself otherwise?"

9. See Eugen Weber, *Satan Franc-Maçon* (Paris, 1964).

10. *Jean Barois* (Paris, 1921), 179: "All the organizers of social leagues, of moral unions, of popular universities . . . all the believers without a church . . . the pacifists . . . in one word, all who have a generous spirit. There is our public."

11. Rolland, *Mémoires*, 34-35. In 1885, already, Ernest Dupuy had written on the *Grands maîtres de la littérature russe*. But the success was for Vogüé who, in 1888, was elected to the French Academy.

12. Geneviève Bianquis, *Nietzsche en France* (Paris, 1929), 46-47.

13. Their concern with Dreyfus is no excuse. Opponents like the men of the Action Française, of the *Revue critique*, were just as concerned as they and yet found time for him. See Reino Virtanen, "Nietzsche and the Action Française," *Journal of the History of Ideas*, XI, 2 (April, 1950), 191-214; *La Cocarde*, March 7, 1895; Weber, *Action Française* (Stanford, 1962), 73-81, *passim*.

14. Harry Alpert, *Emile Durkheim and his Sociology* (New York, 1939), 35; Kurt H. Wolff, *Emile Durkheim*, 1858-1917 (Columbus, 1960), 25. Further, *L'Ennemi des lois*, 166.

15. *Jean Barois* (Paris, 1921), 180; Durkheim, *Le Socialisme* (Paris, 1928), 297; Henri Peyre in Wolff, *Emile Durkheim*, 29-30.

16. Bourget, *Le Disciple* (Paris, 1911), 7, 8, 9.

17. Vogüé, *Lettres*, July 30, 1886, p. 137. For *Le Disciple's* influence, see especially Théodor de Wyzewa's introduction to the 1911 edition of the book, and Victor Giraud, *Les Maîtres de l'heure* (Paris, 1914), 277, 282-83.

18. Rolland, *Le Cloître de la rue d'Ulm* (Paris, 1952), 199.

19. Jean de la Harpe, "Souvenirs personnels," in Albert Béguin and Pierre Thévenaz, *Henri Bergson* (Neuchâtel, 1943), 359.

20. Marcel Raymond, "Bergson et la poésie récente," in *ibid.*, 285-86; *Essai*, 11; compare Barrès, *Sous l'oeil des barbares*, 46.

21. Bergson, *Laughter* (London, 1911), 150-51, 155-56. The theme of this essay was first sketched out in a lecture Bergson delivered in the 1880's, while still at Clermont-Ferrand, and then reworked for publication in the *Revue de Paris* of February 1, 15, and March 1, 1900. At that time he referred to the revelatory quality of artistic creation, mentioning particularly, the impressionist masters of the moment's image: Monet, Verlaine, and Debussy. To non-artists, however, the invention of the artist can serve only as a secondary source for their own revelation. Art is a precious suggestion, but aesthetic intuition can be achieved only by direct contact with reality.

22. See George Mosse, "The Mystical Origins of German National Socialism," *Journal of The History of Ideas*, 82.

23. Junod, "Roses de Noel," Béguin and Thévenaz, *Bergson*, 50-51; Georges Duhamel, *Biographie de mes fantômes, 1901-1906* (Paris, 1944), 50; Gilbert Maire, *Bergson, mon Maître* (Paris, 1935), 143.

24. *Un Homme libre*, 203.

25. *L'Illustration*, July 31, 1886; Barrès, Preface to the 1904 edition of *Un Homme libre*, xi.

26. *L'Illustration*, February 5, 1887; Rolland, *Le Cloître*, 118, 174-5 and *Mémoires*, 277-78.

27. Louis-Hubert-Gonzalve Lyautey, *Lettres du Tonkin et de Madagascar, 1894-1899* (Paris, 1920), I, 49; Charles Maurras, *Au Signe de Flore* (Paris, 1933), 44.

28. John Bowditch, "The Concept of *élan vital:* A Rationalization of Weakness" in Edward Meade Earle, *Modern France* (Princeton, 1951), 32-43.

29. *Un Homme libre*, 100-01; Georges Hardy, *Portrait de Lyautey* (Paris, 1949), 310.

30. *Nouvelle Revue*, v.108-09, 1897; *Revue des Deux Mondes*, January 1900; *Jean Barois*, 325-27, May 1900.

31. Marcel Pagnol, *La Gloire de mon père* (Paris, 1957), 21-28 and *passim*. There are few more moving vignettes of the *instituteurs* of the Third Republic. But see also George Duveau's perceptive chapter "Les Saints sans espérance," *Les Instituteurs* (Paris, 1957), 111-58.

32. See the case of Raymond Poincaré, born in 1860, who also lost his faith when he came to finish his studies in Paris, also hesitated between a journalistic and a literary career, serving his apprenticeship on the *Voltaire* at the same time as his compatriot, Barrès. In 1886, his literary, journalistic, and legal endeavors provide little satisfaction and less income. A family friend, becoming Minister of Agriculture, appoints him his *chef de cabinet*, then other relations bring him into the Chamber. Such are the uncertain beginnings of a great career.

33. Vigreux, *Etudes sur le marché financier* (Paris, 1951), 169-72; Fritz

Sternberg, *Capitalism and Socialism on Trial* (London, 1951); Jean Lhomme, *La Grande Bourgeoisie au pouvoir* (Paris, 1960), 331.

34. Lhomme, *op. cit.*, 276; René Rémond, *La Droite en France* (Paris, 1954), p. 146.

35. Rolland, *Mémoires*, 253, *Une Amitié française* (Paris, 1955), 42-43; Jacques Suffel, *Anatole France par lui-même* (Paris, 1954), 52-54; Emile Pouget, *La Confédération générale du travail* (Paris, 1908), 41-42, quoted Bowditch, *op. cit.*, 34-35; Verhaert in *Le Mouvement socialiste*, IV (1900), 713 ff, quoted Georges Weill, *Histoire du Mouvement social en France, 1852-1902* (Paris, 1904), 454.

36. *Nouvelle Revue*, November 15, 1881, 398: *"Toute oeuvre d'art est une action. . . ."*

THE TORTOISE AND THE HARE

1. Anyone who has read *Being and Nothingness* will perceive the extent to which Valéry's idea and vocabulary in this passage anticipate Sartre's description of the *pour-soi*. Jean Hippolyte was the first to notice the unexpected resemblance. ("Note sur Paul Valéry et la crise de la conscience," *La Vie intellectuelle*, March, 1946.)

2. An earlier treatment of this theme appears in *An Evening with Monsieur Teste*. Of this text about another "master of his own thought," Valéry later wrote: "I think there is also in it a kind of transposition out of art and a unification of Leonardo da Vinci and Mallarmé." The figure of Descartes also lurks behind both figures. The best treatment of the literary and philosophical value of these two works by Valéry is in Francis Scarfe's book.

3. The most thoroughgoing criticism is Meyer Schapiro's "Leonardo and Freud: An Art-Historical Study," in *Journal of the History of Ideas*, April, 1956. So far as I know no one has undertaken to correct Professor Schapiro's extreme position in two matters. Freud did not accept Pfister's "discovery" of a vulture hidden in the St. Anne painting as confirmation of his theories. The 1919 note says the discovery "is of remarkable interest, even if one may not feel inclined to accept it without reserve." And the one new document Professor Schapiro cites about Leonardo's ten godparents supports his own thesis of a hostile mother no more strongly than Freud's. Both these matters arise at the start of the article; the remainder of it and the conclusion seem to me very judicious, and his documentation invaluable.

4. A passage often quoted from *Note et Digression* runs thus: "I sensed that this past master of all disciplines, this adept at drawing, at illustration, at mathematics, had found the central attitude from which the undertakings of knowledge and the operations of art are equally possible; the exchange between analysis and action, singularly probable: a marvellously exhilarating mind."

In the years to follow, Valéry did not remain alone. In the *Second Surrealist Manifesto* André Breton writes as follows in 1929: "Everything leads us to believe that there exists a certain vantage point of the mind, from which life and death, the real and the imaginary, past and future, the communicable and the incommunicable, high and low, cease to be perceived as contradictory. Now, it would be useless to look for any other motive in surrealist activity than the determination of this point."

5. The burning question of how "savages" think has begun to provide a focus for such varied disciplines as linguistics, anthropology, psychology, taxonomy, logic, literary criticism, and mathematics. Some recent and general treatments: Claude Lévi-Strauss, *La Pensée sauvage*, Paris, 1962; Aimé Patri, "La Pensée Sauvage et la notre," in *Preuves*, February, 1963; and the group of articles in *Esprit*, October, 1963.

FRIEDRICH MEINECKE, HISTORIAN OF A WORLD IN CRISIS

1. A complete bibliography of Meinecke's writings may be found in Richard W. Sterling, *Ethics in a World of Power, The Political Ideas of Friedrich Meinecke*, (Princeton: Princeton University Press, 1958), 301-16. Of the fast growing literature on Meinecke only the most important can be mentioned here. Besides Sterling: Ludwig Dehio, *Friedrich Meinecke* (Berlin, 1953); Hans Rothfels, *Friedrich Meinecke* (Berlin, 1954); Walter Bussmann, *Friedrich Meinecke* (Berlin, 1963); Walter Hofer, *Geschichtsschreibung und Weltanschauung, Betrachtungen zum Werke Friedrich Meineckes* (München, 1950).

2. Klemperer, in *American Historical Review* LXVIII, No. 3, 741.

3. Quoted by Carlo Antoni, *From History to Sociology, The Transition in German Historical Thinking*, English translation (Detroit, 1959), 86.

4. Gerhard Masur, "Friedrich Meinecke, *American German Review* XX, No. 5, 1954.

5. Friedrich Meinecke, *Erlebtes, 1862-1901* (Leipzig, 1944), 15-82.

6. *Ibid.*, 81; 176. Antoni, *op. cit.*, 88.

7. Meinecke, *Erlebtes*, 176.

8. Friedrich Meinecke, *Das Leben des Generalfeldmarschalls Hermann von Boyen*, 2 vols. (Stuttgart, 1896-99). See also Antoni, *op. cit.*, 90.

9. Friedrich Meinecke, *Weltbürgertum und Nationalstaat, Studien zur Genesis des deutschen Nationalstaates* (München, 1908). Friedrich Meinecke, *Das Zeitalter der deutschen Erhebung* (Göttingen, 1957).

10. Gerhard Masur, "Max Weber und Friedrich Meinecke in Ihrem Verhältnis zur politischen Macht," in *Studium Berolinense* (Berlin, 1960), 702-25.

11. See Friedrich Meinecke, *Erinnerungen, 1901-1907* (Stuttgart, 1949), 90 ff, 101.

12. Friedrich Meinecke, *Radowitz und die deutsche Revolution* (Berlin, 1913).
13. Friedrich Meinecke, *Die deutsche Erhebung von 1914* (Stuttgart, 1914); Friedrich Meinecke, *Politische Schriften und Reden*, ed. Georg Kotowski (Darmstadt, 1958), 76 ff.
14. Meinecke, *Politische Schriften*, 206 ff.
15. Meinecke, *Erinnerungen*, 240 ff.
16. Friedrich Meinecke, *Die Idee der Staatsräson in der neueren Geschichte* (München, 1924). A new edition has been published by Walther Hofer in 1957. An English translation by Douglas Scott appeared under the title *Machiavellism: The Doctrine of Raison d'État and its Place in Modern History* (New Haven, 1957).
17. So Hofer in his introduction to Meinecke's work, *op. cit.*, p. XIX.
18. See the review of Scott's translation in the Literary Supplement, *Times* (London), December 6, 1957.
19. Ernst Troeltsch, *Der Historismus und seine Probleme* (Tübingen, 1922). Friedrich Meinecke, *Die Entstehung des Historismus* (München, 1936); a new edition with an introduction by Carl Hinrich was published in 1959. Antoni, *op. cit.*, 84. H. Stuart Hughes, *Consciousness and Society* (New York, 1958), 229 ff.
20. See also, Friedrick Meinecke, *Zur Theorie und Philosophie der Geschichte*, ed. Eberhard Kessel (Stuttgart, 1959), especially, 215-379.
21. Gerhard Masur, *Prophets of Yesterday* (New York, 1961), 89-97.
22. Antoni, *op. cit.*, 116. See also Leonard Krieger, "The Horizons of History," *American Historical Review* LXIII, No. 1, 68.
23. Sterling, *op. cit.*, 3.
24. Meinecke, *Politische Schriften*, 426 ff.
25. Friedrich Meinecke, *Ausgewählter Briefwechsel*, ed. L. Dehio und Peter Classen (Stuttgart, 1962). The volume is a moving testimony to Meinecke's human and political convictions.
26. Friedrich Meinecke, *Die deutsche Katastrophe* (Wiesbaden, 1946); English translation *The German Catastrophe*, by Sidney B. Fay (Cambridge, Mass., 1950).
27. Fritz Störi, "Geschichtsschreibung und Weltanschauung im Werk Friedrich Meineckes," *Neue Züricher Zeitung*, July 4, 1953; Walther Hofer, "Friedrich Meineckes," *Neue Züricher Zeitung*, October 27, 1962. Gustav Schmidt, *Deutscher Historismus und der Übergang zur parlamentarischen Demokratie* (Lübeck und Hamburg, 1964).

DIALOGS ACROSS THE CENTURIES: WEBER, MARX, HEGEL, LUTHER

1. Max Weber, *The Protestant Ethic and the Spirit of Capitalism*, trans. Talcott Parsons, with a foreword by R. H. Tawney (New York: Charles Scribner's Sons, 1958), pp. 181-82.

2. *From Max Weber: Essays in Sociology*, ed. and trans. by H. H. Gerth and Ç. Wright Mills (New York: Oxford University Press, paperback, 1958), p. 155.

3. *Ibid.*, p. 156.

The author wishes to acknowledge the influence of previous work on this theme by Karl Loewith and Talcott Parsons, particularly the "Structure of Social Action." He also invites attention to his own essays, "Herbert Marcuse on Max Weber" (*Proceedings* of the German Sociological Society, 1964); "In defense of Max Weber" (*Encounter,* August 1964, 95-96); and "Max Weber's Protestant Ethic and the Spirit of Capitalism, 1904-64" (Forthcoming).

REFERENCES

Clark, Kenneth. *Leonardo da Vinci*, Cambridge, 1939.

Du Bos, Charles. *Approximations*, Paris, 1922.

Freud, Sigmund. *Standard Edition of the Complete Psychological Works*, London, Hogarth Press, 1957 (Vol. XI contains *Leonardo da Vinci and a Memory of His Childhood*, trans. Alan Tyson).

Huyghe, René. "Léonard de Vinci et Paul Valéry," *Gazette des Beaux-Arts*, October, 1953.

Hytier, Jean. *La Poétique de Valéry*, Paris, 1953.

Jones, Ernest. *The Life and Work of Sigmund Freud*, Vols. I and II, New York, Basic Books, 1953, 1955.

Morgenau, Henry. "The New Style of Science," *Yale Alumni Magazine*, February, 1963.

The Notebooks of Leonardo da Vinci, trans. Edward MacCurdy, New York, Reynal and Hitchcock, n.d.

Poincaré, Henri. *La Science et l'hypothèse* (1902); *La Valeur de la science* (1904); *Science et méthode* (1908).

Séailles, Gabriel. *Léonard de Vinci*, Paris, 1892.

Scarfe, Francis. *The Art of Paul Valéry*, London, 1954.

Schapiro, Meyer. "Leonardo and Freud: An Art-Historical Study," *Journal of the History of Ideas*, April, 1956.

Valéry, Paul. *Œuvres*, Vols. I and II, Paris, Gallimard, 1957, 1960.

The manuscript was edited by Elvin T. Gidley. The book was designed by Richard Kinney and the cover was designed by Robert LeVeque. The typefaces are Linotype Times Roman designed by Stanley Morison in 1932 and Venus, cut 1907-1913 by Bauer and based on a 19th century design.

The book is printed on Allied Paper Company's Paperback Offset Book. The paper edition is bound in Champion Paper Company's Texcover and the hard cover edition is bound in Joanna Mills' Parchment cloth. Manufactured in the United States of America.